# Reviews for
# "How I Made Money Using the Nicolas Darvas System"

Steve Burns wants you to follow the trend and make money. That is a good thing. Listen up! – Michael W. Covel, bestselling author of "Trend Following" & "The Complete Turtle Trader"

Awesome work! This quick read is full of golden nuggets of market wisdom and I encourage everyone to learn from those who have been this successful...Darvas and Burns alike...this is a must read to add to any trader or investor's arsenal! – Timothy Sykes, author of "An American Hedge Fund"

Go read Steve's book, "How I Made Money Using the Darvas System." It's a fast read, purposely kept as simple as possible, so that even total newbies can understand it. And, it shows a real-life example of how you can use the Darvas System to make big money and truly change your life for the better. – Darrin Donnelly, "DarvasTrader.com"

This book is powerful because it simplifies a subject that many people find hard to understand. This book offers people a clear strategy for becoming financially free. – Keith Cameron Smith, Author of "The Top 10 Distinctions between Millionaires and the Middle Class"

This book is essential reading for Darvas followers. I have read all of the Darvas books in print and Steve Burns' book not only uses all Darvas' techniques but compliments and confirms what Darvas has done using real examples and making real money. – Fred Chen, Amazon.com Reviewer

This book reminds us all that it's not enough to make money in the market, if you don't keep the money you make. Steve Burns gives time tested and life tested instruction in how to make sure you keep the money you make in the market. – C. Oliver, Amazon.com Reviewer, Vine Voice

# New Trader, Rich Trader

*Also by Steve Burns:*
*How I Made Money Using the Nicolas Darvas System*

For information regarding special discounts for bulk
purchases, please contact BN Publishing at
sales@bnpublishing.net

# New Trader, Rich Trader:
# How to Make Money in the Stock Market

*By: Steve Burns*
*With Janna Burns*

# Contents

## Introduction

The purpose of this book is to share with readers the principles of successful trading: methodology, risk management, and psychology. New traders usually learn these the hard way, by losing money.

**When a new trader enters the stock market with money but no experience, the odds are he will quickly gain experience by losing money.**

This book was written to give new traders a head start in the markets. With only about one in 10 traders actually making money in the market, I believe this book can increase these odds substantially. It is critical to begin trading with a sound methodology which gives you an advantage over the markets. But even more important is the trader's ability to take losses and persevere through the rough education that will ensue. You will be competing with other traders whose only goal is to make money. Profits are made by being on the right side of the trade. Unfortunately, new traders find themselves on the wrong side of trades the majority of the time when they are first starting out. Make no mistake: it is a journey worth taking. The profits are there for those who follow the right principles, manage their losses, and run their trading like a business. Successful traders made it because they persevered through the initial losses and learned how to win in the long term. In this book I share with you the lessons I learned in the markets over the past 12 years. These lessons come from many sources. I learned many of these lessons and principles from my own personal experiences of winning and losing. I also have read and studied over 150 books on investing and trading. I have friends and mentors who have been an inspiration with their successes and who I learned a great deal from. I also have picked up many powerful principles from reading books written by great traders about their methods of success. This book is meant to be a shortcut to the principles necessary to be a successful trader – without having to trade for a decade, spend thousands of hours reading, or learn the hard way by losing thousands of dollars. It is my hope that you find this book helpful and useful on your trading journey. I wish I had it when I began trading.

## Foreword

I was thrilled when I first heard Steve Burns' story.

First off, here was someone who not only survived one of the worst periods in the history of the stock market, but he actually traded his way to a six-figure fortune during this period.

But beyond the fact that Burns thrived during such a tough investors' period, I loved learning that he was just a "regular guy" trading with his retirement account. He wasn't some Wall Street big shot who managed other people's money to make his fortune, and he wasn't some type of financial academic who looked back on the rocky market and offered a hypothetical model of what an investor should have done.

No, Steve Burns was like most people. He had a job, a family, and a mortgage to worry about. He was simply interested in securing his own financial future with wise investment decisions.

But Burns was unlike most people in that he didn't blindly follow the traditional buy-and-hold "Wall Street wisdom," and he didn't trust his money in the hands of others. He took charge of his financial future by studying what actually worked and implementing his strategy in the simplest way possible.

Burns found his investment method of choice in the trendy trading strategy known as "The Darvas System." This system was invented in the late 1950s by a successful ballroom dancer (read: non-Wall Street professional) named Nicolas Darvas who used his strategy to turn $30,000 into more than $2 million in less than two years. The Darvas System implements a simple charting method for riding the upward trends of big-earning growth stocks and then exiting positions when the trend is broken.

While the Darvas System has evolved a great deal over the past 60-plus years, it has remained, at its core, a very simple way to trade stock trends: you buy a great stock when it breaks out of its top base, you hold it for as long as it remains in a steady uptrend (ignoring the "normal" pullbacks along the way), and you sell it when it finally breaks its uptrend. This very simple and proven theory is actually quite difficult for most people to follow due to the human emotions and psychological barriers which come with holding a stock during a long uptrend despite pullbacks.

The keys to successful trend trading are removing your emotions from the trade, avoiding the Wall Street "noise" and stock guru "predictions," and keeping your buy-and-sell rules as simple, clear, and easy to implement as possible.

Steve Burns has mastered the keys to successful trading, and in this book he reveals the rules, techniques, and lessons that are essential to trading success.

If you're new to the stock market, understanding these rules will save you years of frustration and painful losses. If you're a seasoned pro, consider this the "commandments of trading" that need to be repeatedly pounded into your head.

I believe that anyone who wants to earn big money trading stocks (or steadily grow their nest egg without losing big money) should keep this book on their desk at all times. I see it as an essential handbook of trend trading, and I believe a generation of traders will be very thankful that Steve Burns took the time to write this wonderful book.

Darrin Donnelly
*Editor of DarvasTrader.com*
March 2011

# PART I
# Psychology

# 1

**New Traders are greedy and have unrealistic expectations; Rich Traders are realistic about their returns.**

When New Trader awoke, bright and early, he could feel his excitement building with every moment.

Booting up his computer, he couldn't help but remember every excruciating detail that went into building his account, the many hours of overtime at his regular job and delivering pizzas on weekends to earn some extra cash.

But now that part of his life was over. His heartbeat quickened as he typed in his username and password for his $10,000 account.

He was ready.

How could he not be? New Trader had been trading through simulated accounts for over a year, watched CNBC, and followed many trading gurus.

The way he saw it, it was easy.

When an account lost too much money, he simply opened up a new one. And when he made a great return, his selective memory decided to forget the account that had lost so much...

This fed his ego, convincing him that he could easily outperform the market.

New Trader projected that he could double his account in a few months, then do so again by the end of the year, bringing his account to $40,000.

It wouldn't be so hard, he thought; he had read a few books about legendary traders, so now all he had to do was repeat what they had done.

Unfortunately for New Trader, he either didn't read or

didn't comprehend the fact that these very same traders suffered losses and faced difficulties before their amazing successes.

Many had blown up, losing 50% or more of their starting capital. Some even went bankrupt when they didn't control their risk or broke from their trading plan.

But unfortunately, New Trader, who was still high on the excitement of his shiny new $10,000 in buying power, could not conceive any loss. His excitement overruled any fear or doubt that may have entered his mind.

New Trader was eager and hungry to trade, quickly familiarizing himself with the tools. All of these were new to him: the charting software, the real time streamers, how to enter trades.

So now there was only one question left: What to trade?

First he would need a stock that would double to help him reach his first goal, or trade a stock for a 26% return three times.

He knew the math; he was always great at math in school and was used to always finding solutions to problems.

Trading was simply math. And math was simply logic. New Trader was logical.

Or so he thought, as his head swam in the results of compounded returns; he would be a millionaire in a few years, just like his trading heroes!

Actually, one of his heroes, Rich Trader, lived in the city. New Trader found himself frequently going to the man with questions about how to become a trader...perhaps he should ask him for some last-minute advice before he started trading... not that he needed it, of course!

And that was how New Trader found himself knocking on his mentor's door. They exchanged their usual greeting and

Rich Trader let him in.

"I suppose this is about that account of yours?" Rich Trader said with a wry smile. This wasn't the first time New Trader came to Rich Trader's home about the account.

"I really appreciate you being able to answer my questions," the younger man said as Rich Trader poured himself some freshly brewed coffee, getting New Trader a mug as he listened.

"My plan is…" New Trader began speaking as soon as the coffee was in his hand, "…to double my account in a few months, then double it again so I can build it up to 40,000 to trade with next year… what?"

Rich Trader was looking at him with an amused grin.

"Wow…" he took a sip of coffee. "So you're planning to be one of the top traders in the world the first year you trade? That's a very aggressive goal… for a beginner."

"I just need to find a stock that doubles twice, or have 26% returns compounded six times!" New Trader said, in the overeager exuberance Rich Trader had come to expect from him.

Rich Trader shook his head, the wry smile back on his lips as he removed his glasses and rubbed his eyes, as if in thought.

"Well, New Trader," he said after a moment, "while those returns are possible, they usually only happen during special time periods – like the booming late '20s bull market, or the Internet stock boom of the late '90s. Historically, certain ultra-high growth stocks like Cisco, Google, or Apple did perform very well for long periods of time, but those are very special stocks, and not only do you have to pick these stocks, but you have to have the right plan to buy and sell at the right time; your hot stock could just as easily fall 50% instead of doubling…"

He paused, taking a breath.

"Not only that, but the market would have to trend in favor of your style for you to make such outstanding returns. It doesn't do you any good to plan to buy a stock that's going to double if the market turns bearish and the stock falls. In a downturn in the economy, or when fear takes hold of investors, they tend to sell just about everything and move their money where they think it will be safe. Sometimes this means consumer staple stocks, but sometimes it will be bonds or even commodities like gold or oil."

When Rich Trader put his glasses back on, he saw that New Trader's hopeful expression had fallen into one of confusion.

"So you're saying I may not get my 200% return this year?" New Trader asked.

"There is a high probability you will lose money this year," Rich Trader replied in a matter-of-fact tone.

"But… I didn't go through all the trouble of saving money and opening an account to lose; my only purpose is to win," New Trader responded, voice full of pride.

Rich Trader sighed.

"The market will teach you many lessons before you consistently make money – the most dangerous thing you can do is make a great deal of money from the start. That usually leads to recklessness and losing big long term."

"Isn't that what I want to do, win big?" New Trader asked, incredulous.

"No, you want to get rich slowly. You want to make consistent returns over a long period of time; your account can grow rapidly by compounding your gains. While you're doing this, you have to manage your risk for minimum draw downs in your equity. Successful trading is based on ever-increasing account equity with minimum draw downs. Properly managing your account also sets you up for those trades that will return 25% during a trend or for the year you do have a 200% return. **Your first job as a trader is to focus on trading, not profits,"** Rich Trader said, taking a sip of his coffee.

"Okay... so if I do focus on trading, what returns can I expect?" New Trader asked, curious.

"Realistically, a good trader can get a 20% to 50% return or more a year. However the odds are a trader loses money the first year, but gains an education. You have to look at it like paying tuition. Trading is a profession like any other, and you are trading against professionals most of the time. A doctor doesn't just read a book and start practicing medicine; he must go to medical school to learn the proper procedures from other doctors. He also will have to make mistakes before he gets paid to be a doctor. With doctors, hopefully their mistakes are made in medical school and not on a patient!"

Rich Trader looked at New Trader, who was listening studiously.

"Trading is no different." He continued, "I would also assume there's a huge difference between operating on a corpse and on a live person during surgery. I am sure there is a real factor of stress that comes into play in the operating room, and the doctor must manage stress and have confidence in his performance and his ability to follow the correct procedures. A doctor doesn't think about how much he's getting paid while he is performing surgery. You need to focus on a sound strategy, style, and trading plan – not profits. Good trading will create your profits, while focusing primarily on your profits will likely lead to bad trading."

New Trader could feel his agitation and disappointment growing. This advice might have been good for some other beginner, but he was different. He was sharp and had a better feel for the market than others did. He was the exception.

When he finally responded, it was difficult to hide the snide tone from his mentor.

"So you think I could make a 50% return, or $5,000 in profit this year, and that would be realistic and possible."

Rich Trader could obviously sense his attitude, but it didn't seem to bother him.

"I think that would put you in the top 1% of all traders. The question is: are you willing to do the work to beat the other 99%?" Rich Trader asked.

"Of course I am!" New Trader replied, even as he felt his hold on the dream of easy money loosening.

**"People who look for easy money invariably pay for the privilege of proving conclusively that it cannot be found on this earth." – Jesse Livermore**

**Recommended reading for this chapter's lesson:**

The Universal Principles of Successful Trading: Essential Knowledge for All Traders in All Markets, by Brent Penfold

## 2

## New Traders make the wrong decisions because of stress; Rich Traders are able to manage stress.

New Trader had been watching his stock all morning.

It had gone from $9.25 to $9.55 and then back to $9.45 – he loved watching the volume change to higher and higher numbers. He loved watching his stock glow a brilliant green while the others fell red.

The Dow Jones was red, and the NASDAQ was clutching to green by just barely a tenth of a percent.

Now his stock was $9.40, and now he was ready.

He wanted a thousand shares.

He had $10,000 in his account, and he knew this stock could easily rise to $12.00 over the next two months, giving him $2,600 profit.

He decided to get in at $9.25; it was showing strong support at $9.00 and hadn't been below that in weeks.

It had over the past month been around $9.03, but reversed and rallied on high volume before it hit $9.00. In the past month, it had also reached as high as $9.89 but stalled there at a new all-time high.

As the price fell to $9.30, then $9.25, New Trader felt a rush of excitement as he quickly keyed in the stock symbol, and '1000' beside quantity.

His heart was racing as he clicked on his mouse again to see the current positions. Glancing at his account screen, it showed:

1000 shares SRRS BUY Executed $9.35

"$9.35?!" New Trader exclaimed, shocked.

Looking back at his real time streamer, his blood froze as he saw the current quote: $9.10.

He felt sick.

"I... just lost $250?! It takes me an entire weekend of delivering pizzas to make $250," he muttered, fear tightly gripping his stomach.

His heart was pounding, though this time it was from fear, not excitement.

Looking back at the quote, he saw that according to the daily high and low prices, the stock had fallen all the way to $9.08. But it was now at $9.15. He tried to calm himself.

"It will hold at $9.00, then turn around and get to $12.00 before earnings. I got a great price to buy in at," he said to himself.

Paper trading and simulations was one thing, but this was different. This was his money – every cent came from his blood, sweat, and tears, and to have $250 snatched away just like that...

It felt like he'd just been robbed.

Why wasn't it going the way he planned? This pressure, stress, and fear were nothing like what he had expected... especially for such a small drop in price.

While he was pulling himself together, the stock rose to $9.40, yet it didn't calm him down, despite the $50 in profit.

He still felt gripped by fear, and he wavered on whether to take his profits or to do as he had originally planned and hold until earnings in the next four weeks.

It was as though he could physically feel every penny of his $10,000 perilously crossing a tightrope without a safety net. It was like his $10,000 could fall into oblivion at any moment. He had never been in this kind of real danger before, and he didn't understand it.

With shaking fingers, New Trader called his mentor, who answered on the third torturous ring.

"Hello?"

New Trader began to feel ashamed, certain that his reactions would seem silly to Rich Trader. Even so, he managed to force out the words.

"I placed my first trade."

There was a pause, and New Trader could swear the older man was sporting one of those amused smiles.

"That's good..."

"How do you control your stress when trading?" New Trader asked so quickly his mentor could barely understand.

New Trader heard a deep chuckle that grated on his nerves – how can he be so calm?!

"Most stresses arise from unknown variables – fear of loss, uncertainty of market trend, or the need to make money. Sometimes traders allow their ego to get so wrapped up in a trade that their self-worth gets wrapped up in the need to be right," Rich Trader replied easily.

"But how do you control stress?" New Trader urged.

**You can limit your stress level by removing as many unknowns as possible from your trading.** You should know your trading plan before you start trading. You should already have a watch list of what you'll buy. You have to decide how many shares of what specific stock to trade even before you execute the trade."

Rich Trader cleared his throat and continued.

"Before you place the trade, you need to have in place an exit strategy of how, when, and why you will take profits and what your stop loss will be. You have to plan to sell your stock at a specific percentage loss, price support breach, or trend change."

"Well, I suppose that makes sense."

"All traders experience stress and must manage it like in any other job. If your stress level is still excessive after you have a working trading plan, then you are either trading too big or don't have faith in your trading system. If you know your system is a winner in the long term, then try cutting your position size in half. If 1,000 shares stress you out, try trading 500."

"But..." New Trader started, before silencing himself so Rich Trader could continue.

"If you're still overwhelmed, go down to 400 or 300 shares per trade. If you believe your stress is caused by not having faith in your system, then you need to back-test your strategy. Depending on your system and its complexity, this may require back-testing your buy-and-sell signals with computer programs or with past charts. You can also test your trading method by simply trading your exact entry and exit signals on paper or in simulators; you will need at least 30 trades over different types of markets to get a real feel for your win/ loss statistics."

"So I need to make sure I have a system that I follow. Then I need to design a trading plan with which I'm comfortable trading. Then I have to test my system to ensure it's a winner, so I can develop faith in my strategy and limit my stress. If I still feel too much pressure, I can just decrease my trading size until I'm comfortable."

"Yes, exactly; you need to have a plan to control the outcomes of what's in your power to control – like stop losses, trailing stops, position size, timing, and technical indicators. You will need to be comfortable with the volatility of the stock you are trading. Traders need a trading style that's compatible with their personality. Aggressive types like a stock that moves and gives them huge profit potential. Others like a nice steady stock they can trade at predictable price support and resistance levels. Some love the activity of day trading, while others prefer systems which only require adjustments a few times a month. The important thing is that you are trading a system you that is comfortable to you and that is profitable. If you are stressed to an unhealthy level, then your lack of faith in your system or your lack of confidence in your knowledge or abilities are the cause; alternatively, you may simply be trading too big of a position for your comfort zone."

"I see... you sound like you're speaking from experience."

Rich Trader laughed again.

"Well, I understand now. Thanks again for taking the time to talk to me."

"Oh, it's no trouble," Rich Trader replied.

Now New Trader felt as though he had a better understanding. A thousand shares were obviously too much for him, but now he knew what he had to do.

**"If you experience high levels of stress during trading, either you are trading too big of a position or you do not have enough confidence in your system. Reduce your position or do further testing on your system to cure your stress." – Steve Burns**

**Recommended reading for this chapter's lesson:**

Enhancing Trader Performance: Proven Strategies from the Cutting Edge of Trading Psychology, by Brett Steenbarger

## 3

## New Traders are impatient and look for constant action; Rich Traders are patient and wait for buy signals.

New Trader woke two hours before the stock market opened, excited about finally having a day off to trade.

He made a strong cup of coffee to prepare for the day, signed into his computer, and began to look at the market action in Asia and Europe.

All markets were up a nice half a percent on the major indexes. His stock SRRS was at $9.70 in pre-market trading.

He grinned.

I'm up $350 in just one day; I really have a talent for trading...

But first things first: I must reduce my position size to what I am comfortable with and create a trading plan that follows a profitable system.

As the market opened he sold 500 shares of SRRS for $9.75 a share. He made $200 in capital gains minus $10 for the commission to trade in and out of the stock.

He was very pleased with the $180 in profits on his first trade. He was still holding the 500 shares of SRRS to go into earnings with, and was aiming at his $12 price range.

He felt a sense of relief with a stock position of less than $5,000 instead of one closer to $10,000.

He wasn't experiencing the accelerated heart rate or stress he had felt at 1,000 shares, and concluded that 500 shares or $5,000 should be his size per position.

He was hoping, however, that as his experience and account grew he would be more comfortable with bigger trades. Time would tell.

Now he felt like he had to get the money in his account

back to work.

Since his account was a margin account, he could trade with this money today and not have to wait three days for the trade to clear, as others with cash accounts for trading must do.

He felt much more comfortable with a 500-share position of $5,000, which was to be his trading plan. If a stock was $50 he would trade 100 shares. If a stock was $5, he would trade 1,000 shares. He also figured he might have to factor in the volatility of a stock.

He wanted to trade stable stocks in up trends. He would trade stocks with no more than a 2% to 5% daily price range. He then went online and checked his stock SRRS for its price history.

It was a volatile stock, just barely averaging less than 5% a day in price movement.

This didn't stress New Trader; he wanted a stock with movement. He needed some volatility to show him the movement of the trend, to make a profit, and to cover his trading costs.

He began asking himself questions to build his trading plan. With CNBC playing in the background and his live streamers flashing on the computer screen, he settled in to think.

He glanced back at his position; his stock was now at $9.92; it had broken through the 52-week high.

This made him happy. He felt a sense of satisfaction having picked a winner and having purchased it at a good entry point.

But then he thought: why exactly did I buy at that price? Was it because it was a short-term price support? Was it a hunch? Did he really have a system that he traded, or was he merely a discretionary trader, trading on his opinion?

He had trouble finding answers to these questions. At the same time he had a strong desire to put the other $5,000 in his account to work in a trade.

He looked at his watch list for action. The overall market was now up almost 1% across most indexes, and DMY, a supplier to SRRS, was at a new 52-week high of $4.90.

He didn't think; he just bought 1,000 shares at $4.91 of DMY. The stock then went to $4.95, then stalled and reversed to $4.92. He was hoping for a strong trend up for profits.

While he was watching the Bid/Ask spread hang around the $4.92/$4.93 area for a few minutes, he questioned himself:

What am I doing? I have no exit strategy. I don't even know why I bought the shares.

He didn't realize it at the time, but greed was his motivator – and in the future it would ask him to make some bad decisions. But for now he was just confused.

Maybe creating a trading plan during trading hours was not the best decision.

With the stock going nowhere after 30 minutes of staring and straining at the screen, he decided to sell. He sold 1,000 shares for $4.92.

Good thing I didn't lose any money on that trade…

On closer examination, however, he noticed his account had $10 less value than before the trade.

His profit was $10 but he had to pay $20 in commissions on the trade.

Now he just felt foolish for having made that trade, and to do it while trying to create a trading plan seemed ridiculous to him.

He decided to call Rich Trader.

When Rich Trader answered the phone in his normal, pleasant voice, New Trader wasted no time. He got right to the point.

"Have you ever made a trade without knowing why you did it?"

"Yes, when I was much younger, in the heat of battle, when the stakes were high and the adrenaline got going, I did things I regretted."

"What causes overtrading or spontaneous trading?"

"I would say this particular problem is caused by a few different things:

1. Not having a specific trading plan.

2. Being bored and looking for excitement.

3. Being arrogant and thinking you can trade just based on being smarter than other traders."

*"And what can I do to stop this?"*

"I would suggest that you **trade only to make money, not for entertainment or to prove anything about yourself.** Much of the time profitable trading is boring. If you already know what you are going to do before you trade, that takes a lot of the excitement out of it. If you trade with a system that gives you an advantage in the market and have a trading plan on exactly how you will trade your system, then there are no spontaneous trades. You are waiting for entry signals and exit signals. In time, as you suffer losses on trades you make based only on your opinion, you will come to learn that **your system makes you money in the long term but your ego loses you money in the short term. Trade your system, not your opinions.**"

"That makes a lot of sense…"

"Do your planning and research while the market is closed; trade your system while the market is open."

"I still have a lot to learn. Thanks for listening."

"Experience has always been the greatest teacher," Rich Trader replied.

New Trader decided it would be best to not make any more trades until he had a plan.

**"It is better to do nothing than to do what is wrong. For whatever you do, you do to yourself."– Buddha**

**Recommended reading for this chapter's lesson:**

Trading for a Living, by Alexander Elder

## 4

## New Traders trade because they are influenced by their own greed and fear; Good Traders use a trading plan.

New Trader felt more prepared than ever before. It was time to get serious; it was time to start creating a trading plan. But first he had to answer some questions.

Taking one of his favorite trading books off the shelf, he opened it to the chapter on how to write a trading plan.

What will be your signal for entering a trade?

When will you sell?

How much will you risk on each trade?

What will be your trade size?

What equities will you trade?

How long will you hold your trades?

How will you test your system for profitability?

What is your ratio of risk to expected reward?

And so he started making decisions.

I'll trade trends, he thought, so my signal needs to buy into price and volume strength.

So instead of buying support, he would buy either at the break to a new high, or when it breaks resistance of either a moving average or price.

He decided to risk only 5% of his trading account per trade. This would greatly reduce the risk of ruin he had read about so many times before. So if he traded a $5,000 position, he would only risk $250 total; with a 500-share position that would be 50 cents a share. His stop on his SRRS trade should be at $8.85, since he bought it at $9.35 and still had 500 shares.

When do I plan to sell SRRS?

If I have a stop loss I need a plan to take profits.

Twelve dollars was his target, but what if it only goes only to $11.99 and then reverses? Would he be ridiculous enough to give back his profits and maybe even lose money if it kept falling, even below his purchase price?

He thought the best plan would be to trail a stop loss and take profits if it pulled back 5%. If it went up steadily to $9.85, then pulled back to $9.35, he would get out even.

If it went all the way to $11.99, then pulled back to $11.19, he would get out with a nice profit. He would avoid giving back all his profits and have a plan to sell.

The stock, however, would have to have a nice uptrend for this system to work. In a bull market, he knew, it should do very well.

It would allow profits to run nicely and prevent too many stop losses when the stock just moves in its normal price range.

So he decided that his trade size would be $5,000 and how-ever many shares that buys for a particular stock.

He would trade in the hottest stocks in the market, with at least one million shares traded a day for liquidity. They would have to have a daily range of less than 4%.

This would alleviate being stopped out because of volatility.

Not only that, but the best stocks can run up to 15% or more before earnings – some can even go up 50% or even double before their trend changes.

This would give him a chance to cash in on the big winners, but his buys would need to be prompt. He couldn't afford to give up 4% in an uptrend, then chase the stock and buy it late. In a volatile stock which moves a lot during the day, it would be crucial that his stock was in an uptrend and didn't pull back 5% and get him stopped out.

So he decided he should put in a buy stop so that the stock would be automatically bought at the beginning of an uptrend.

His plan was to hold stocks as long as they go up without pulling back by 5% in price. A price breakout could fail, forcing him to sell on the first day and make him a day trader. Or he could also end up holding a stock for over a year as it never pulls back 5% and just rockets up and doubles. He would put 5%, or $250, at risk in each trade with unlimited upside.

The only ways to test his system was to paper trade or use a simulator; but his stock picking was too subjective and discretionary to program into software.

New Trader felt confident in his trading plan. He had simply followed suggestions from the many trading books he had read and the advice of Rich Trader. He didn't feel the need to bother Rich Trader again.

Haven't I bothered him enough?

He was beginning to feel like a businessman writing a business plan. This was feeling was quite different from the adrenaline rush he got from trading on his opinions.

For a moment he wondered if his plan was not aggressive enough. He should be taking more risk. Was $250 a trade really worth all this trouble?

His greed wanted a much more aggressive trading plan; it wanted to be a millionaire in a year, not trade for a few hundred dollars.

As greed tempted him into a more aggressive trading plan, fear began to gnaw at him. He could feel doubts rising in his heart and mind.

What if I lose my first ten trades in a row? That will be

$2,500 gone; I worked hard for that money. It could take me four or five months to save that much again!

He felt nauseous.

"Was it worth it?" he said aloud, thinking about his job, then his second job.

He thought about the legends he had read about who had made millions, and the freedom that Rich Trader enjoyed. Rich Trader had a nice home and had no job to report into. No boss, no schedule – he had become a millionaire even though he was a college dropout!

So New Trader had a decision to make.

Would he just give up and go back to working at a job for the rest of his life, or would he continue on his journey to wealth?

At once the choice seemed so easy to make. He would be a trader. What other job offered this kind of opportunity and these odds for success? It was like a lottery he could eventually win based on hard work and learning the business.

He would continue on his journey, experiencing both fear and excitement as he continued to grow and learn.

**"Pride is a great banana peel – as are hope, fear, and greed. My biggest slipups occurred shortly after I got emotionally involved with positions." –Ed Seykota**

**Recommended reading for this chapter's lesson:**

The Psychology of Trading: Tools and Techniques for Minding the Markets, by Brett Steenbarger

## 5

## New Traders are unsuccessful when they stop learning; Rich Traders never stop learning about the market.

New Trader woke up feeling like he had finally done it.

He was a good trader. He had his style and his trading plan.

He called New Trader to see if he was available for brunch – it was Saturday, so the markets were closed.

So what does a trader do? Relax and enjoy his profits.

They agreed to meet, and before noon they were sitting in a homey restaurant ordering their favorite breakfast foods. They relaxed and settled in for a delicious meal.

"I have this trading thing figured out," New Trader said out of the blue while enjoying his eggs.

Rich Trader choked on his orange juice, almost making a scene with his boisterous laughter

"What's so funny?" New Trader asked, bewildered by Rich Trader's reaction. This was serious business!

"I-I'm sorry," Rich Trader said as he finally caught his breath, "but that was…" He laughed again, though it was more of a chuckle, "I don't think I've ever heard anyone say that before."

"I've done a lot of research, and decided on my style: trend trading. I've also written my trading plan," he said, handing Rich Trader a folded piece of paper, then eating a slice of bacon.

Rich Trader looked it over carefully. "This is a great start."

"Start?" New Trader said incredulously, frowning as he finished off his second piece of bacon.

"This is like your first freshman paper you're turning in for your first class. If you're like other successful traders you will have to test this system first and then make adjustments."

Rich Trader took another sip of orange juice.

"It may work well for a while, then suddenly stop working and give your capital a large draw down due to a change in market conditions. The system may not even work; you don't know yet. Or it might make you a nice profit in a bull market then take the profits back in a bear market. If you want to be profitable in a bear market, you may have to reverse your system and sell the same stocks short when they break down through support. Testing your system both in simulations and real money will teach you a lot. You first need to get an idea of your winning percentage and the average sizes of your wins and losses."

New Trader could feel the confidence he had when he walked into the restaurant wilting. Why did trading have to be so complicated?

He felt his appetite dwindle into nothingness after Rich Trader's lesson, and disappointment settled on his shoulders. He hadn't even considered the possibility that his system would be only the beginning and not the end of his homework and study.

It seemed this meeting with Rich Trader wouldn't be as different as he thought – he always came confident but left humbled.

"So my next step is system testing and making adjustments?" New Trader asked, attempting to hide his deflated ego.

"Yes, your system is built on solid principles, but you need to quantify and measure them as much as possible. You need to build a record of how the system performs in real trades. But most importantly, you need to test your discipline and confidence in trading the system exactly as you planned," Rich Trader informed him, taking a bite of pancakes.

"Of course I will!" New Trader said defensively.

Rich Trader raised a brow, amused.

"I would also strongly suggest keeping a trading journal where you list your trades; list your plan before and after the trade. Record any problems you have in your own ability to buy or sell at the right times according to your trading plan and system. Record breaches of discipline and why you traded off the plan. You have to always be watchful for an inflated ego taking over your trading, and the emotions of greed and fear. Boredom can turn good traders into bad traders as they look for action instead of profits. **A trading journal is like having a teacher who teaches traders about themselves.**"

New Trader bit back his first reply – that it was silly and a waste of time – but he knew Rich Trader had his best interests at heart and had yet to steer him wrong.

And he didn't want to feel the fool again after not doing it.

"What would my journal show me?"

"Patterns."

"What kind of patterns?"

"Patterns in what causes your good trades and your bad trades. What you were thinking and what caused you to go against your plan? Also, what made your best trades possible? You might even see patterns that show your system works best in the morning or in the final two hours of trading. You should pack as much information as possible into your journal, along with your actual trade information, your mood, feelings, goals, and even your charts with buy and sell areas marked, if possible."

"I'll do that then," said New Trader as he picked at his last pancake. The fact that he didn't have an appetite for his favorite pancakes was unsettling enough.

"Are there any other lessons you think are important?" New Trader asked dejectedly, yet hopefully.

"Always stay humble. Always know the market is too big for anyone to master. You must never stop learning about yourself, about the market, and about risk," Rich Trader said before posing a question, "How many trading books have you read?"

"Ten," New Trader said, hoping it wasn't a disappointing number.

"Most of the best traders have read hundreds," Rich Trader said, and New Trader sighed. He was expecting that somehow.

"How long do you spend looking at charts each day?"

"A few minutes before I place a trade..." New Trader said sheepishly. He knew that wasn't a good answer...

"Great traders spend hours a day doing homework on charts, identifying support, resistance, and trend," Rich Trader informed his student gently. "Great traders are life-long learners. My advice is to always be a student of the market, always go to bed each night understanding more about the market than you did when you woke up. With hard work, experience, and focus, you will one day convert all that time into money."

**"In my whole life, I have known no wise people over a broad subject matter area who didn't read all the time – none, zero." – Charlie Munger (Warren Buffet's partner at Berkshire Hathaway)**

**Recommended reading for this chapter's lesson:**
How Legendary Traders made Millions, by John Boik

# PART II
# Risk

## 6

## New Traders act like gamblers; Rich Traders operate like businesspeople.

New Trader turned his alarm off as soon as it started its annoying bleeps – he had been lying awake for some time, but now it was an hour before the market opened and he needed to prepare.

He could feel an unusual amount of adrenaline as he always seemed to before he traded, and he rushed to turn on CNBC.

The European and Asian markets were up over 1%, and though he tried to understand the numbers they were spouting off, he couldn't decipher exactly why the markets were up. But he knew that the traders were bullish and prices were headed up.

And so, confident he would be making money that day, he laid his trading plan beside his computer. He spent two weeks after that breakfast with Rich Trader testing his system on a simulator and had recorded the 10 test trades.

Trade 1: -$250
Trade 2: -$250
Trade 3:  $250
Trade 4:  Even
Trade 5:  $500
Trade 6: -$250
Trade 7:  $200
Trade 8:  $750
Trade 9:  $300
Trade 10: $400

With seven wins and three losses (when you don't lose money it's a win; you only have to pay the expense of the commission), he had made $2,400, and lost $750, for a profit of $1,650.

His system seemed to work well, but he knew Rich Trader would tell him it took more than ten trades to define a system's long-term viability, and that the market being in an uptrend could be a factor other than the system itself.

He looked at his journal – glad that he had taken Rich Trader's advice – to refresh what he had learned.

1) Cutting losses was crucial; many of the stocks I sold with a $250 loss continued to fall and I could have lost over $1,000 on one. I must know the amount of money I am willing to risk before I trade.

2) Buy stops are good because it helped me make extra money on the move by getting into a trade automatically. If I would have attempted to buy some of these stocks in an uptrend, I would have lost hundreds of dollars in profits while trying to manually buy it as it shot upward.

3) I take a profit when it begins to fall. If I didn't have a trailing stop I would have given back all my profits on two of the trades. It's good to have a profit-taking strategy.

I think my system could be better if I find a way to buy earlier in a hot stock, maybe at support, and take profits on a big run up instead of on a draw down. I'm sure Rich Trader will have some advice.

New Trader felt a strong pull to trade in the markets that morning, so he decided to scan his watch list for buy points.

His greed was like a little devil on his shoulder, whispering in his ear, telling him to buy the stock in his real account instead of the simulated account.

He deserved it, didn't he? – said the little devil. He had worked hard, learning about trading and building his account. He deserved the profits. The market owed him.

The real-time streamers flashed red and green, tempting him in the way that Las Vegas lights tempt gamblers. For a moment the little devil won, and the delusion of winning big, easy money sat in his mind.

He was clever, after all – the little devil known as Greed told him – and he could beat the market.

Stocks were going up; he only had his one SRRS position on; it was now at $10.35, and he had paper profits of $500. That was encouraging, and he would sell if it retraced to $9.85.

His rational mind returned as he looked down at his trading plan and realized he had to stay on track. It would be foolish to wildly buy a stock with no plan. It was time to get away from the computer – and the temptation to trade.

 He eventually called Rich Trader and received an open invitation to come for a talk.

When New Trader showed up around noon, he suddenly realized that he never saw Rich Trader watching CNBC, nor did Rich Trader have a fancy trading station.

*Does he even still trade? Is he retired?*

"I am really surprised at the temptations I feel when I trade," New Trader began. "I keep wanting to trade aggressively instead of following my plan."

"Like all businesses and disciplines, the psychological aspect is usually the part that causes people to become unsuccessful," Rich Trader said. **"Being a professional means doing your job no manner how you feel.** A trader really has two jobs – you are both a researcher and a trader. First you must do your research; find systems that have a good probability of success in the long term, test those systems, and create a trading plan that fits your personality. Measure the best amount of risk to take on each trade based on your winning percentage and historical drawdown. Then your next job is to follow this plan and not change it during market hours. Adjustments should be made in off hours."

"Draw down?" New Trader asked, feeling a bit foolish.

"In trading, an account does not go straight up. You may start with $10,000, go down to $9,500, then go up to $10,500. Even if you double your account it may be a choppy uptrend. You may have a big win followed by three small losses then another big win, then two small losses. That's normal. **The key to success is to lose small and win big,**" Rich Trader said. "When you're in a loser, get out; the best trades make money at the buy point. When you're winning, let it run until it stops. The best way to lose quickly is to not cut losses, hoping they will come back as they fall farther and farther, or to take quick profits and miss the big profits that pay for your losses."

"There is also one more, very important, thing," Rich Trader added after a moment. **"When you go to your computer to trade, you should approach it as if you are entering an auction, not a casino.** You should feel like you are going to work for your own business, not like you're going to pull a slot machine or put down chips on a number on the roulette wheel. If you experience these feelings or you just want to gamble, you will eventually fail at trading. "

"Trend traders make money, chart readers make money, swing traders make money, day traders make money, and position traders make money, but all gamblers in the market eventually lose everything."

When Rich Trader finished, New Trader felt a little unsettled but took the warning to heart.

**"Risk comes from not knowing what you're doing."** – **Warren Buffett**

**Recommended reading for this chapter's lesson:**
Trading without Gambling, by Marcel Link

7

## New Traders bet the farm; Rich Traders carefully control trading size.

New Trader was deep in thought.

He wanted more profits and he wanted them to come more quickly.

Perhaps with his experience holding 500 shares of SRRS for almost a month he was ready to trade 1,000 shares. He would just have one position of $10,000 instead of two positions of $5,000.

Now that he had $20,000 with the use of margin, surely he would be comfortable trading $10,000...

He thought it through over and over, trying to convince himself to change his trading plan. He wanted a big trading account, and he wanted it as quickly as possible.

He was just so sure that SRRS was going to twelve by the time its earnings were announced, and he was so very tempted to go all in.

Of course, at this point Greed was getting the better of him. He was conscious enough of the fact, and knew he needed to concentrate on Rich Trader's lessons.

**"Your first job as a trader is to focus on trading, not profits."**

Profits would come to him one trade at a time. Then a thought flashed: SRRS $11 call options for next month were trading at $1 a contract, and so the crazy thought entered his head.

I could control 10,000 shares for my $10,000.

He knew that option contracts were for 100 shares, and that the quote price is for each share that he would control; so paying $100 to control 100 shares was rather simply understood.

What he didn't understand was that the stock had to not only go up to $11, but to $11 plus the cost of the option premium. SRRS had to go up to $12 in 30 days just to break even.

He wasn't buying intrinsic value, just $3 in time value with the stock trading around $10. He was buying the right to the shares at that price for one month.

He didn't understand how very slim the possibility of the stock moving up 20% in 30 days would be.

Historically, SRRS moved between 10 and 15 percent leading up to or after each earnings announcement – which had already occurred.

New Trader was tempted into a trade that had five major problems:

1. It was against his trading plan.

2. He did not fully understand the nature of what he would be trading.

3. He had not researched the history of the stocks price action to understand the probability of the trade being successful.

4. It was an all-or-nothing bet. If the options expired worthless he would lose his entire account of $10,000.

5. Even if he was right and made huge profits on this trade, it would encourage him to take the risk again. This would lead to eventually losing his entire account.

Fortunately for him, his trepidation caused him to listen to another of his emotions – Fear.

Many times this emotion can cripple a trader, but it is still wise to have enough to ward off Greed.

Fear was very quick to point out that he could lose everything if this trade was a complete lost. It also prevented him from calling Rich Trader to tell him about his compulsion to roll the dice and bet the farm.

Then something dawned on New Trader:

**If I am too embarrassed to talk a trade over with my trading mentor, it's not a trade I should be doing.**

New Trader decided to go to his mentor's home for advice on making his trading plan better – and more suited for his goals. But he also decided not to tell Rich Trader about his bout with Greed.

He arrived at Rich Trader's house unannounced in the middle of the weekday and was surprised to see him in pajamas with a book he had obviously just been reading.

How... odd.

Why was the TV off? Why wasn't CNBC on? Why wasn't the computer whirring with Rich Trader glued to the screen?

New Trader was curious.

"Are you doing any trading today?" he asked, as he stood awkwardly in the doorway.

Rich Trader raised a brow as he motioned New Trader inside.

"I have some trailing stops in, so if my positions reverse I'll be sold out. I'm going to check in at the last hour of trade to see if I should enter any additional buy stops."

New Trader was dumbfounded.

He just couldn't understand how Rich Trader, with an account his size, and doing this for a living, could possibly be so blasé about his trading.

Why wasn't he staring at every tick and wanting to know every little thing about the markets?!

"Aren't you concerned about your positions or about missing any trading opportunities?" New Trader asked, as he entered the living room.

"Well, we all hate to lose money, but my sells are based on hitting predetermined stop losses and not my opinions. I also trade a system, not my opinions about what the market will do. So there's no need to be glued to my computer and CNBC since it could cause me to be impulsive and take trades against my trading plan."

"I was tempted to take a trade against my trading plan today but chose not to," admitted New Trader sheepishly. Whatever happened to not telling Rich Trader?

"Well, the most dangerous part of your plan to violate is your risk. Trading a larger position puts your account at great risk," said Rich Trader.

"That's… actually what I was tempted to do."

Rich Trader shook his head.

"If you make a mistake and lose a few percentage points of your account, that's not as big a deal; you can trade and get that back. You can lose 5% of your account four times in a row and be down 20%, so you need five wins in a row to get back 25% to be even again." He paused in thought. "Of course, normally these are spread out like two wins a loss, then three wins and two losses, et cetera. The problem begins when you take one big reckless trade with a bad stop loss plan and lose 50% of your account; you must gain 100% to get back to even. If a 50% loss takes your $10,000 account to $5,000, you need to gain 100% on your new $5,000 in capital to get back to $10,000. That is a disaster. If you go from $10,000 to $8,000 with a 20% loss, a 25% return will take you back to $10,000. The greatest determiner of your risk is the size of your trade. I would never risk more than a 4% loss on any trade. Good trades are generally ones which show a profit from the beginning."

"I was going with 5% as my stop loss and percentage of risk."

"And what is your expected gain for your wins?"

"I don't know."

Rich Trader sighed. "That's very important information to have. Out of ten trades, if you take a 5% loss five times and your 5 wins are only 2.5%, you are still down 12.5% on ten trades that are evenly sized. If you lose 5% five times, however, and then gain 10% five times, you are up 25% after ten trades that are the same position size with a 50% win rate. However if you do not keep consistent position sizes you will distort your payoff ratio."

"Payoff ratio?" New Trader said with a confused expression.

"Basically, the ratio of the average winning trade to the average losing trade. The larger this ratio is the better chance for having a winning strategy. It's difficult to be a successful trader with a payoff ratio under 1.5. The ratio is calculated by dividing the gross profits by the gross losses. Most traders want at least $2 of reward for every $1 risked. Which is what the 5% loss versus 10% win scenario with a 50% win ratio gave you in our second example. As you test and trade your system it is crucial to keep track of your winning percentage and payoff ratio so you can set up profit expectations. It's also crucial to develop faith in your system to be able to continue trading it when it is losing. All systems go through draw downs when market conditions are not conducive to profits based on the style of your system."

"Hmm... I see. Thanks again, Rich Trader. You've definitely opened up a new area I need to examine carefully while I develop my system and trading plan... I have a lot of work to do..."

"Anytime, New Trader," said Rich Trader, picking up his book again as he showed the younger man out. "But next time, would you mind calling first?"

New Trader gave a wry grin.

"Throughout my financial career, I have continually witnessed examples of other people that I have known being ruined by a failure to respect risk. If you don't take a hard look at risk, it will take you." – Larry Hite

Recommended reading for this chapter's lesson:

A Trader's Money Management System: How to Ensure Profit and Avoid the Risk of Ruin, by Bennett McDowell

## 8

### For New Traders huge profits are the #1 priority; for Rich Traders managing risk is the #1 priority.

First thing the next morning, New Trader was knocking on Rich Trader's door. Rich Trader opened the door after a few minutes.

"Hello, again," Rich Trader said in his usual, pleasant tone. "You called this time at least."

New Trader grinned. "Of course… I've come for class, Professor."

"Well, then. I'm afraid I don't have a lecture prepared today, but why don't you come in, have a seat, and tell me about what you're curious about. Perhaps I can help."

"Well… risk seems to be a much deeper – a more important topic than I thought it would be."

"Risk is like a Cerberus, and it can bite a trader many different ways. Different trading methods expose you to different kinds of risk."

"I thought risk was just the chance that you could lose money…"

"It is, but there are many ways you can lose money:

1. You have the basic risk that your trade will be a loser, that it will move in the opposite direction of your long or short position. This is **trade risk;** however most times you can control the maximum amount you lose through position size and a stop loss.

2. You also have the **general market risk** factor. You can pick a stock of a wonderful company but if the trend of the stock market itself is down for some reason, the likelihood is that your stock will also fall regardless of the

fundamental merits of the company or the past strength of your stock's price movement. The market is like a tide that comes in, lifts up all ships, and then goes out and lowers them back down.

3. You have the risk of your stock either being or becoming highly volatile. **Volatility risk** can scare you into selling your stock too soon or simply cause your system to stop working because the stock you bought hit your predetermined stop loss and forced you to sell – even though it might reverse and be right back where it started later that same day. It is the broadening of a stock's price range from its past history.

4. **Overnight risk** is when something unexpected happens while the market is closed and the next morning your stock gaps down in the pre-market and you never even had a chance to sell and stop your loss. This risk applies to everyone except day traders or traders who trade markets that are open 24 hours.

5. **Liquidity risk** is when there are just not many buyers or sellers for your stock, so you lose money in the bid/ask spread. The "bid" is what a market maker is willing to buy your stock for, and the "ask" is what they are offering to sell it for. There are stocks and options which have such low volume that you can lose 5%-10% just simply buying and selling, even if the stock price does not move. If your stock has a BID $9.50 and ASK $10.00 and you buy it at the ask price then sell it at the bid price, you lose 5% when you enter and exit the trade. It is important to trade in stocks that have a small spread in the bid/ask quotes. Less than 10 cents is good but a penny or two is excellent.

6. **Margin risk** is when you use your stocks as collateral and borrow money from your broker to buy additional stocks. Most brokers, after you have set up a margin account, will allow you to buy additional stocks and dou-

ble the size of your account. With margin you can use a $10,000 account to buy $20,000 worth of stock as long as the stocks are marginable securities. Some more risky penny stocks and small cap stocks are not marginable. The good thing about margin is you make twice as much profit when you are right, but the risk is that you can lose twice as much if you are wrong. Doubling your risk with margin greatly increases your risk of ruin by making your losses compound twice as fast!

7. **Earnings Risk:** If you are holding a stock through earnings, you are exposed to the risk of a sharp move in one direction after the announcement. It can hurt your account if the move is too fast after hours and blows through your stop loss.

8. **Political Risk** is a possibility if you are invested in a company located in a different country or your stock's company does a majority of its business in a country that suddenly has a change in power. Investors and property owners of all kinds were wiped out when the Communists took over all private property for the state in Cuba in 1960.

9. **Time decay risk:** If you trade options, the clock is always ticking against you. A major component of a stock options value is its time value: each day it loses a small amount of this value until it is only worth its intrinsic worth – how much it is 'in the money' based on its strike price. So if you decide to trade options, you must be right about the price movement and the timeframe. You are also paying for the right to control the shares, so you have to be right by more than the cost of the option for it to be a winning trade.

10. There is also the **risk of error** where you can actually put one too many zeroes on the amount of shares you want to buy for a trade, or buy the wrong symbol, or sell

a stock short instead of buying it long. Double checking your trades before you place them is very important.

11. One of the most frustrating kinds of risk of all is **technology risk.** If trading is not hard enough already, you can also have your Internet connection crash or your broker's trading platform go down while you are in a trade. These are good reasons to have a backup plan like the phone number for your broker ready at the push of a button to get out of a trade entered. Anything can happen while you are trading, so be prepared."

When Rich Trader finished, New Trader took a moment to let it all sink in and finish his notes before replying.

"That's... a little overwhelming. It's amazing to me that you can speak about all that off the top of your head."

"As a trader you quickly learn to respect risk. Before you start any block of trades you have to look at all the risks involved. Ask yourself questions like: 'How much am I willing to risk per trade?' and 'If I lose five times in a row what will be my percentage of drawdown?'"

"Can you give me any suggestions on managing these different types of risk?"

"Here are some simple suggestions to help lower your risks when you trade. Some of this you have probably heard before:

**1.** Determine your stop loss before any trade is placed.

**2. Honor your stop; CUT YOUR LOSS.**

**3.** Trade the same size of dollar value in every trade to even out your losses with your wins.

**4.** Only take trades that meet the criteria of your predetermined trading plan.

**5.** Trade mostly long in up trending bullish markets and

mostly short in down trending bearish markets. (A 10-day moving average over the 20-day moving average is a good sign of an uptrend, and the reverse is a sign of bearishness).

**6.** Only use margin to trade more trades of equal size. On margin you do not typically have to wait three days for your trade to clear and you can keep trading after trades are closed. Do not use margin to make one huge trade.

**7.** Only trade in stocks with over a million or more shares traded a day and options with open interest of over a thousand contracts.

**8.** If you decide to be a day trader you can avoid overnight risk, however the most profitable traders carry trades for weeks and months. The only ways to manage this risk is to either become a day trader wherein there is a huge amount of uncertainty in the markets, or you can simply go to cash when a huge announcement is set after hours, whether it be political in nature or simply earnings for your company.

**9.** To manage the risk of volatility you can simply trade slow, dependable stocks which have consistent daily ranges. A stock with a beta of 1.0 simply moves the same as the S&P 500; a stock with a 2.0 moves twice a fast as the index. You want to trade lower beta stocks to manage volatility. You do not need a volatile stock to make money; you just need a stock that is either in a trend or in a price range with support and resistance levels.

**10.** You can control political risk by simply trading stocks that do the majority of their business in countries with historically stable governments, such as the United States, Great Britain, Canada, Japan, etc. When you trade in emerging markets you take on the element of political risk.

**11.** If you do trade options you can limit the risk of time decay by trading deep in the money calls and puts. Most of these are pure intrinsic value and do not even have much time value, if any. Some of these options move close to 100% with the stock price. So even though they cost more, you eliminate the risk of time running out before they go in the money.

**12.** Remember to always double check trade information before you hit that last trade button. I have accidentally traded 10,000 shares instead of 1,000. I have also accidentally traded a stock long when I meant to short it. This is a real risk like any other.

**13.** Have a Plan B for your broker and Internet connection. I always keep my broker in my 'contacts' on my cell phone, and I also have the Internet on my phone to check stock prices."

"I never really thought about all the risks involved. Those are a lot of good points to think about when writing a trading plan and picking stocks for my watch list. Thanks for my lesson of the day. I'm sure it will be of great value to my trading," New Trader said, prepared to leave and continue his journey of becoming a trader.

"Of course, I am always happy to help," Rich Trader said pleasantly, his throat a bit sore.

**"Rule #1: Never lose money. Rule #2: Never forget rule #1." – Warren Buffett**

**Recommended reading for this chapter's lesson:**

Super Trader, by Van Tharp

## 9

### New Traders try to prove they are right; Rich Traders admit when they are wrong.

New Trader stumbled sleepily to his computer.

He had been holding SRRS for over a month now and it had been behaving well; the stock had climbed up to a new all-time high of $10.58 before going all the way back to $10.03.

He was quite proud of himself and confident his stock would rise to $12 as he predicted.

He turned on his computer lazily, still not completely awake. A few clicks later and he was in his brokerage account, clicking on his real-time streamer, getting up to fix some coffee.

And then his stomach dropped.

$9.25.

The pre-market quote was $9.25! Forgetting even the thought of coffee, he was now wide awake.

"$9.25? What the…"

He quickly worked through the math. At one time he was up $615, and now he was down $50?! His profits had evaporated – overnight.

He searched the Internet for answers and found that one of SRRS's rivals had announced that it was bringing an electronic device to the market that was superior to SRRS's. Analysts believed it would be available in less than four months and that it would take 20% market share over the first year from the SRRS product.

New Trader could feel his mind shut down, but not before his ego took over his trading plan.

What do I do now?

Don't worry, his Ego soothed, you're right… hold the position. The stock will come back… The other company's product can't be as good as the original – this is just a natural reaction from other traders…

He was right, New Trader agreed, his ego not accepting this small loss in the stead of the huge gain he was expecting.

He couldn't bear to think of all the hard work he'd done these past months – for what seemed like nothing. All the wasted time and effort and frustration…what was the point? Was it worth it? If he didn't sell, he wasn't wrong – not yet. He would just have to be patient for the rally.

Then he would sell.

That's what his Ego said, in any case. His trading plan simply said: "Sell."

New Trader's trading plan – unlike his Ego – was neutral. It was based on New Trader's rationale.

The trading plan was created to dictate what to do through the lens of New Trader's methodology and system. It was meant to protect New Trader from huge losses or from giving back too much of his profits.

Unfortunately, New Trader believed he was smarter than the trading plan. He barely remembered he had planned to sell when the stock retraced 5%.

This stock had retraced over 10% and he still wasn't convinced to sell.

The trading plan was not his boss when he was looking at the loss of $615 in paper profits. He was attached to them; he had been fawning over them daily for weeks. They were his, and he would get them back.

His Ego was 100% behind him. It shouted "Don't sell, wait for it to come back, at least get out even!"

As New Trader was pondering all of this the market opened. He eagerly stared at the quote. The opening price was $9.30, then $9.20; next quote $9.18, $9.14, and $9.09.

Nausea set in and New Trader's heart pounded against his ribcage as he obsessed over every bid and every ask price, every quote, the volume – it all meant something to him.

But he was viewing each movement as validation that he was right. It would rebound.

Of course it will go down to $9.00, that was support; it cannot go lower than $9.00, and buyers will move in to support it. The volume was not as heavy as it should be if this was a real sell off. He shouldn't sell; this is a great time to buy, why would I sell?

Ego comforted New Trader as more of his money evaporated by the minute.

$8.98 was the last quote. He was now down $185; he was heading into the territory of the most he wanted to lose on any one trade. His inability to honor his stop had now cost him $135 more than if he would have simply honored it and stuck with the plan and sold at the open.

He was sure now there would have to be a bounce; it was right at support, it was oversold. The buyers would be scooping up the bargain.

SRRS made a move to $9.10, then rolled over and plummeted to $8.80 in a manner of seconds; the volume spiked half a day's volume for SRRS and the stock fell like a rock into a deep well.

The pain was too much. New Trader sold out.

It made him sick. He was demoralized.

He felt like a failure both for picking SRRS and for not selling it when the stock opened below his planned stop.

He lost $275 after he had spent so many weeks admiring his $615 profits.

He had wasted so much time glued to quotes for SRRS, watching the price move each hour, pretending he was a big-time stock operator interpreting the chart, volume, and price.

His emotions weighed heavily on him. He didn't want to talk to Rich Trader. He didn't want to trade. He felt like a loser.

He felt like a sucker for believing this trading thing would even work.

These were not his thoughts; these were his feelings making him feel like a failure.

After a few hours of brooding he started to look at his streamer again. SRRS had gone all the way to $8.49 and rallied back as high as $8.97, but it was in a new range that morning with the market pricing ending the dominance of its specialty device.

Would it recover by earnings? No one knew. New Trader did not care; he just wanted to make money. But now he truly understood that the reality was that he could lose money on any trade, but he could control what that amount was. **He learned that if a stock met his exit price, trailing stop, or stop loss, the odds were that he was wrong about the trade.** He should take that signal and get out.

He thought it was sort of like insurance. He realized that he shouldn't be mad when he pays for car insurance and doesn't need it that month. Insurance is simply paid to avoid the risk of ruin in the event that he was to total his new car.

Stop losses and trailing stops protect you from the big drop where the trend never reverses and you just lose more and more money waiting for it to "come back." If he would have been able to stop out during regular market hours he also could have locked in some gains.

He realized that even if he was stopped out and then the stock reversed, he could just buy it back – so what?

He understood why it's important to decide where to place the stop losses to avoid being stopped out unnecessarily. The trailing stop would also need to be planned out carefully to keep maximum gains while allowing the trend to run.

The great thing about this incident was that it taught New Trader a personal life lesson, rather than being told about it by someone else. He was lucky to learn this lesson at such a minimal cost. His plan to buy out all of the call options could have led to a loss of his entire account, or his full 1,000 share position could have cost him twice the loss; instead of a loss of $275 he would be looking at a loss of $550.

He was growing as a trader. He was thinking through what had happened and what he had learned. He was turning into a trader. He was thinking like a trader. He was learning the lessons that all traders must at some point learn before they are successful.

The books he had read, Rich Trader's advice, and his own experiences were coming together.

He did not feel like it at the time, but he was very fortunate.


**"Good investing is a peculiar balance between the conviction to follow your ideas and the flexibility to recognize when you have made a mistake." – Michael Steinhardt**


**Recommended reading for this chapter's lesson:**

The Disciplined Trader: Developing Winning Attitudes, by Mark Douglas

## 10

### New Traders give back profits by not having an exit strategy; Rich Traders lock in profits while they are there.

The trip to Rich Trader's house was much shorter than New Trader had remembered and before he realized it he was stepping up to the porch.

A part of him was happy to receive another lesson from his mentor, while the other part was mortified by failure to follow his system.

He knew his time would be well spent with Rich Trader and that he would emerge wiser – which would hopefully translate into cash.

He had barely rapped on the door twice before Rich Trader opened it, a mug of steaming coffee in each hand, one held out to New Trader.

New Trader took it with a smile of gratitude and couldn't help but notice something about Rich Trader he'd never seen before – his poise.

He looked like the picture of success, even in a polo shirt and slacks. He carried himself with a sense of purpose and intelligence, as though he planned every word or action.

He always seemed refreshed, ready for the new day, and then New Trader knew he wanted to be exactly like Rich Trader. He wanted the freedom, the confidence, and the security.

That's why he traded.

"Thanks for the coffee."

"It's no trouble," Rich Trader said. "Come in."

New Trader followed him into the dining room.

After a brief bout of small talk, Rich Trader got to the point.

"How's your trading been going?"

"Well, every time I think I have it figured out, a curve ball hits me in the face," said New Trader sheepishly with a half smile.

Rich Trader chuckled.

"Yes… I've taken similar hits right between the eyes. It's all part of the education, you see. But you won't ever 'figure out' the market. **You can't predict the markets; you can only react to the signs it gives you.** At least, that's what I've been successful at."

"So what would you suggest is the best way to take profits in a trading plan?"

"That depends on your trading plan, methodology, and system. Trend traders like me tend to take profits when trailing stops are hit, but sometimes we also have sell signals as a stock falls through a moving average support or hits a new low for a certain number of days. We always let profits run as far as possible. We want to give the stock an opportunity to catch the big trends. A trend trader must capture large wins to pay for all the small losses."

Rich Trader took a sip of coffee before continuing.

"However there are traders that trade support and resistance and would sell their stock once it reaches the price they consider resistance. If your system is looking for short-term swings in price like trading around an earnings announcement, you might simply have a target based on the historical price action of the stock."

"What do you mean by 'historical price action'?"

"I mean that if you're swing trading a stock and buying it a month before the underlying company announces its earnings, you would want to know how much the stock moved leading up into earnings announcements over the past year."

Rich Trader cleared his throat.

"If the last four times the stock increased 8%, 7%, 10%, and 12% the four weeks before the company announced earnings, it would be prudent to take profits when the stock was up 7%, or set a stop if it retraces to 7% when it is up 8% or more. If you are up 10% in this particular trade, the odds are that you have all the profits you are going to have and you need to look at taking them."

New Trader paused a moment before replying. "I didn't think about all those moving parts. I was just letting my profits run on my last trade... Then an announcement demolished me in the pre-market. Then to make the problem worse, I didn't sell and take my original loss when it hit my sell target."

"So you had simple bad luck, combined with an overextended profit and failure to follow your trailing stops?"

"Yes," New Trader sighed, "all of the above."

"Well, that was a learning experience. That's also how plane crashes happen; it's never just one problem but a combination that results in catastrophe. It's usually bad weather, a new pilot's error, and a technical malfunction that results in a plane crash. It's never just one thing; there are too many safeguards in place for one thing to cause a catastrophic plane crash, which is much like trading. When you trade you should:

1. Really understand the stock you are trading, its volatility, daily price range, and historical movements leading into earnings. You should also understand how the earnings reports of similar companies affect your stock. Economic reports may also cause movement in your stock. Know it inside-out before you trade it.

2. Control your risk. When a stock moves against you and hits your stop or gaps down below your stop, get out. This is your insurance against ruin. Do not hope, do not try to

predict, just sell. The majority of times this will save you further losses. When you sell you can plan to get back in at a predetermined rally if it fits your trading plan.

3. Keep your Ego out of the trade. Your goal is not to be right every time; your goal is to make money over the long term. This is accomplished by your winners being bigger than your losers. Focus on being right big and wrong small, not on being right every time."

New Trader was writing quickly to help absorb his mentor's advice.

"When you decided not to sell your stock on the gap down, do you know which rules you were violating – psychology, risk, or methodology?"

New Trader frowned.

"I suppose I never thought of the psychology having a lot of rules before, but probably all of the above. My trading plan is based mainly on methodology. Do you have rules for the psychology of trading?"

"I have collected ten principles that have helped my trading over the past twenty years. Every last one of these lessons was learned the hard way."

Rich Trader went to an old notebook next to his computer, flipped the cover open to the first page, and handed it to New Trader. Handwritten on the slightly off-white paper were these ten rules:

1. Read your trading rules and trading plan before trading every day.

2. Never hope for a bounce back; cut losses at predetermined price.

3. Exercise discipline at all times. Follow your predetermined trading plan.

4. Do not overtrade.

5. A successful trade is a trade that follows your trading plan and your system.

6. Do not divide your time; when you are trading, focus only on trading.

7. Your opinion does not matter – only price action.

8. Never try to predict; follow trends and trend reversals.

9. Never fall into the trap of hindsight – only real-time trading counts.

10. Respect the market at all times and do not become arrogant.

"I learned most of these lessons by losing a few thousand dollars violating them. These also came out of my trading journal."

"You know, a few months ago I would have thought this was just common sense and that these rules didn't apply to me, but now I know better and I am surprised at the difference there is between simulated trading and trading live with real money. I haven't started my trading journal. I need to do that too… I need to start acting upon the lessons I wrote down and on the principles and rules you are giving me, which you learned over many years of trading."

"To be successful in anything you have to learn from your mistakes and correct them. If you want to be a great golfer, going and hitting a bucket of balls with the wrong form every day will not make you any better. You need to learn which club to use for different situations, how to hold the club properly, how to swing properly, and also how hard to hit the ball depending on the distance you want the ball to travel. Trading is no different; it is crucial that you learn from your mistakes as quickly as possible and not keep repeating them. The market gives instant feedback to whether you are right or wrong; you need to learn the principles of successful traders. Trading is very rewarding but is not easy. You must have a plan to buy and a plan to sell. Your plan must historically have bigger winners than losers. You must have faith in your plan and continue to follow it even through a few losses in a row. You have to keep your ego in check and not let it take over your trading. You have to keep your risk per trade at a safe point and not get greedy when you have several wins in a row and want to go all in. Trading is a business like any other, and if you treat it like a business you will do well."

**"Take your money off the table while it is still there. Trailing stops = keeping profits." – Steve Burns**

**Recommended reading for this chapter's lesson:**

Sell and Sell Short, by Alexander Elder

# PART III
# Methodology

## 11

**The majority of New Traders quit; Rich Traders persevere in the market until they are successful.**

Lately, New Trader had been doing more thinking than trading.

He asked himself if trading was for him. The answer seemed simple enough.

He loved trading and wanted desperately to make money and be successful. Of course he should continue trading!

And so he decided to search the Internet for the most popular trading books and then visit different web sites which provided free stock charts. He studied the charts to try to understand the price action.

Working with systems that won historically, he traded them with small position sizes to develop track records in real trading.

He was ready to get down to business. He would be successful and it would take study, experience, and perseverance. He was ready to pay the price.

New Trader had a weekend off from work and he was ready to cram his brain full of information. He had a stack of ten trading books next to his favorite reading chair, several financial magazines, his favorite financial newspapers, and plans to visit many web sites.

With a stockpile of sugar, caffeine, and assorted junk food he began his journey at 8 a.m. that Saturday morning.

He flipped his journal open past his documentation of trades and Rich Trader's lessons to a blank page. He would take notes of anything that seemed helpful as he went along.

While looking through chart after chart, he began to see

trends. Most of the time the stock was moving up or down. It might be moving slowly or quickly, and it may have a tight price range or a looser price range, but it was very obvious that the majority of stocks trended.

Moving averages also seemed to play a part in price ranges. He could see what looked like prices literally bouncing off these lines. They had an almost ethereal, yet predictable quality to them.

The 10-, 20-, and 50-day moving averages seemed to be the ones that affected stock prices the most, and when he expanded his charts for very long timeframes and looked at the price action of stock indexes like the S&P 500, Dow Jones Industrial Average, and NASDAQ, it looked like the 100- and 200-day moving averages also came into play.

It also seemed that once a stock or index broke these lines it was hard to get back over them and that this may signal change in the current trend.

It was fascinating.

Stocks of smaller companies seemed to move faster than larger companies. He also noticed large companies were more likely to be range bound than smaller ones.

By studying these charts, patterns started to emerge for New Trader that he hadn't seen before. He spent four hours that morning examining chart after chart.

Bollinger Bands caught his eye, as most of the time it appeared when a stock price would scrape against the top of the bands in an uptrend and the bottom of the bands in a down trend. He looked at the different technical indicators: Moving Averages, Bollinger Bands, MACD, RSI, and Stochastic.

He began to understand charts better, but by noon his stomach told him he needed nourishment. Three slices of pizza and a cola later, he was ready for more research.

He stumbled upon chart patterns on a web site by a respected trader and reviewed each pattern.

He looked at a cup with handles, ascending triangles, head and shoulders, flags and pennants, descending triangles, and wedge formations. He read up on trader psychology theories which were supposed to cause these patterns to form, and he wondered how often they really worked. He also wondered if they could be incorporated into a winning system. He could use these patterns to be a technical trader; he just needed to find what he was comfortable trading.

He was searching for a technique he could trade and develop faith in; he wanted a high percentage winner because he hated losing trades.

A system with a 60% win rate was what he wanted to trade. He wanted his average win to be twice the size of his average loss for a 2:1 ratio of profit versus losses. He knew what he wanted; now he had to find it.

Hot stocks currently in up trends is what really appealed to New Trader so far in his searching and trading.

He liked trading stock that everyone wanted. He liked trading stocks where he understood the company's business, and he liked the market being bullish on his pick.

So far that morning he had learned that **while fundamentals and earnings expectations could tell him what to buy, he needed charts and technical indicators to tell him when to buy.**

The right buy points seemed to be on a pull back to support or a high volume breakout to new highs. The pullback was usually at the 10-day moving average in most of the hot stocks he was looking at.

Some of the super-hot stocks, however, had just been on

an upward tear and never experienced a pull back. They had a breakout on heavy trading volume and never looked back.

Did he really have the guts to trade these breakouts?

He needed rules, and he needed to follow what he decided were the highest probability trades.

Late in the afternoon, he began digging into the trading books.

He read the covers, the table of contents, and about the author. He then began reading each book, reading a chapter or two and then picking up another and reading it for awhile. By evening he had started each book and decided on the five he liked the most, and he continued reading them until midnight.

The principles of trend trading, money management, and chart reading really struck a chord with New Trader. He decided to be a trend trader, looking to profit on trends.

He would use charts to pick his buy and sell point; at this point he was convinced that his opinion really didn't matter. What did matter were the prices buyers were willing to pay for a stock and the price sellers were asking before they would give up their stock.

**Price was reality; personal opinions had little value.**

He started to view the stock market as a democracy with the volume representing the number of votes cast in a particular direction.

Stock prices were not based on a company's underlying valuation. Prices were a composite of all traders' opinions about the future expectations of making money on the stock.

Could fear and greed drive prices more than a company's actual value? This thought was interesting to him; he had never thought about actual price drivers before, but after all the charts and books he had been reading, things started to become clearer.

His head was spinning with thoughts about the markets. He fell asleep in his reading chair with a book in hand. The next morning, New Trader awoke still sitting in the chair, wearing his glasses.

He was excited about the knowledge he was building. He started right back where he had left off in his books. He read all day with only restroom and meal breaks.

He was a man on a mission.

As he went, he jotted down key lessons on growth investing from the trading books which he thought may be important.

- Trade stocks with double-digit-earning increases year over year.
- The general market direction determines the direction of your stock more than anything else.
- Only trade the leaders in the hottest industries.
- Trade stocks which trade at least a million shares a day so they are liquid.
- Stocks that are close to all-time highs and have great support on the charts are the ones to trade.
- Stocks that have new products with heavy consumer demand should have the highest earnings expectations.
- Stay away from illiquid penny stocks; trade stocks on the major exchanges.
- Cut losses at predetermined amounts, 2%-8% maximum.
- Never try to bottom fish or buy a falling stock.
- Never bet against a government taking corrective action in the economy.

Some of this he had heard from Rich Trader, but he picked up many details he hadn't thought about before.

He also had gotten more than halfway through some great

books on trader psychology. By now he knew that having the right mindset would be very important in his trading. He jotted down these lessons:

• <u>You must make up your mind to trade until you are successful, or you may never make it long enough to be successful.</u>

- To win at trading you must think and act like a winner. Whiners are not successful traders.

- The biggest determinant of a trading system's success is the ability of the trader to follow it 100%.

- Listen and learn but also verify the source and whether what is being taught really works.

- Do not start trading real money until you have done due diligence on your system.

- Never trade without a written trading plan.

- Control your trading risk by reducing your risk of ruin to as close to zero as possible while still making an acceptable profit.

- Your system should show your equity curve growing over several months in historical back tests or paper trading.

- Have an accountability partner whom you can talk to about your trading.

- Keep a trading journal with as much detail as possible – how you felt during each trade and what you were thinking. Include charts with buy and sell points if possible.

New Trader was surprised at the many similarities between what he had experienced in his own trading and what the books had to say about the psychology of trading.

Many lessons also reinforced what Rich Trader had been saying. He would continue to read into the night, committed to persevering until he was successful in trading.

**"The harder you work, the harder it is to surrender." –
Vince Lombardi**

**Recommended reading for this chapter's lesson:**

Trading for a Living, by Alexander Elder

## 12

### New Traders hop from system to system the moment they suffer a loss; Rich Traders stick with a winning system even when it's losing.

New Trader decided on Monday morning that his time would be better spent with his mentor.

This would be part of his education in trading, and he figured he could learn what he needed from various sources:

1. A mentor who has been successful in trading for many years.

2. Books, to learn the principles of successful traders.

3. Studying charts to understand repeating patterns.

4. He would also have an accountability partner with whom he could share his ideas and trades to keep himself on track and grounded.

5. He would use journaling to learn about himself and his system as he traded.

This was his plan for success. He was determined to learn and no longer repeat his mistakes.

He knocked on Rich Trader's door and the elder man appeared as quickly as usual. New Trader still didn't understand how he was not glued to CNBC and his stock streamer.

As soon as they were settled in his mentor's house, New Trader blurted out: "Do you still trade? Or did you retire?"

"I still trade, but I use a less aggressive approach," Rich Trader answered.

"What does that mean?"

"I currently trade a trend trading system using stock indexes. The system I am trading is only adjusted in the last hour of trading each day if I get a signal.

"I've always pictured successful traders glued to their computer screens all day, buying and selling, sweating and stressing, watching every news development."

"This is just my personal system right now; it fits my personality and my temperament. There are also day traders and swing traders who actively trade all day and make money doing so. In my opinion, trend trading has been proven to be the most effective way to trade, and trends can last for months. But you can make money in many different ways as long as you follow the right rules. **Disciplined traders can make money trading any system with an edge, but traders without discipline cannot make money trading any system because they will not follow it.** They will try to judge signals instead of following them. They will try to predict the market instead of following what the price and volume are telling them. The really sad thing is that after they take a few small losses they promptly give up, when one of the next few trades is actually the big winner which would pay for all the small losses. The beauty of my current system is that it's very simple and when it catches a trend, it makes large gains with little adjustments needed."

"So you recommend trend trading?"

"I recommend following the principles we have discussed, and trading the style that fits your personality. What are you comfortable trading? Do you want to sit in front of your computer all day and try to scalp small moves in big positions? Do you want to just trade the index and follow the current trend using technical signals like moving averages? Do Bollinger bands appeal to you, using them to buy when the bottom band is reached and sell and maybe even go short at the top band on a chart? You can also be a growth investor, buying the hottest stocks in the market with the greatest earnings expectations and using charts to know when to buy and when to sell. It is like any other career; you will be successful in what you believe in and are passionate about doing."

"I just want to do what makes the most money..."

"The system you follow in a disciplined manner over the long term and that you have faith that it's profitable is the one that will make you the most money."

"What do you mean? The system that I can actually follow will be the one that is most profitable for me? Why do you think I can't follow every type of system that has the best returns?"

"Some people are naturally bargain shoppers; it goes against their very nature to buy a stock or index at an all-time high. They would probably do better to wait for a pullback to a moving average support or the bottom of a Bollinger band. They should still be able to make money with something on their watch list getting a pullback in an uptrend. Another trader may be very aggressive and feel good about buying the breakout because it means his stock has technical power with buyers very bullish on it. This trader will eventually buy a monster stock on his watch list that does not pullback before a huge run which makes him a killing. Both traders will be profitable in the long run because both of them are using systems that work – but it would drive the aggressive trader nuts to wait for a pullback that may not even happen, and the bargain buyer would be sick for paying all-time highs for a stock no matter what it did over the next few days. They will both be uncomfortable with their trades, which will in turn probably render them unsuccessful in the long run. The aggressive trader will lose his patience and buy a stock that has already run too far just in time for the pullback. The bargain hunter will panic and sell stock he deems too expensive at either the first sign of weakness or when it has just begun its run."

"Could you sum up success in trading?"

"Hmm…" Rich Trader mumbled, starting to slowly call out what he thought made him successful in the markets.

"Well, let's see…

1. Find a style of trading you are very interested in and which feels right to you.
2. Learn everything you can about this style.
3. Develop a system that is historically profitable.
4. Develop a watch list of stocks and/or exchange traded funds that have the characteristics which will make them good candidates for your system.
5. Test it out on paper over a few months through different market cycles to see how it currently performs.
6. If you are convinced it is a winning system, begin trading it in very small positions, just enough to be profitable and cover commission costs.
7. Slowly increase your position size as you understand all the moving parts involved in your specific system.
8. Journal your thoughts and feelings as you trade to learn what causes you to over-trade/under-trade or not follow your system.
9. Continue to learn and grow by reading books written by successful traders.
10. Continue to network with seasoned traders to grow as a trader.
11. Discuss your trading with another trader to keep yourself on track."

These were not Rich Trader's opinions, but rather what had made him a millionaire a few times over. Many of his traits were shared with the legends of trading whom he had studied and learned from.

Rich Trader continued.

"As a new trader, you are like a medical intern, sampling all the fields of medicine to see what fits. You should spend some time day trading, swing trading, position trading, trading growth stocks, and trend trading. You should develop a watch list of fast and slow movers; it should include big and small caps index ETFs and leveraged ETFs. You should follow your interests and experiment on paper and in small positions. Listen to your emotions as you trade. Your stress may be telling you that a volatile stock moves too fast for you to deal with. Your boredom may be telling you that the system you are trading is not giving you enough of a return to make it worth your time. Your uncertainty in a trade may be telling you that you have not looked at its historical performance sufficiently to have faith in it."

"So I'm looking for my system, not just a system that makes money?"

"If your trading system does not fit your tolerance for risk and reward, and you cannot develop faith in its performance, then the odds are against your success."

"You can measure the success of your system with these." He pulled out a blank work sheet and explained each line to New Trader.

1. The winning percentage: wins divided by total trades

2. Pay off ratio: Profits versus losses

3. Your largest winning trade

4. Your largest losing trade

5. Average winning trade

6. Average losing trade

7. Largest percentage drawdown: The most money you have lost in a row divided by your starting capital before the

draw down

8. Average percentage drawdown: What is the average money lost during your losing streaks divided by your account before each loss, then divided by number of total losses?

9. Largest numbers of straight losses

10. Largest numbers of straight wins

11. Total percentage profit for different time periods

"These records will build your faith in your system, after 100 trades you should begin to see patterns of how your system performs in different market environments. You may also see flaws which you can adjust to make it perform better, such as a wider trailing stop or how it works best on specific stocks, et cetera. The point is to continually work toward building a trading system which matches your beliefs about the market, which has an advantage you can verify, risks you can control, and a system in which you can develop faith and have the tenacity to follow long term to build your trading capital."

**"Everyone has a game plan 'till they get punched in the mouth." – Mike Tyson**

**Recommended reading for this chapter's lesson:**

How to Make Money in Stocks, by William O'Neal

## 13

## New Traders place trades based on opinions; Rich Traders place trades based on probabilities.

New Trader was buzzing with excitement: Rich Trader had invited him to go to dinner.

This was a first, and he felt he was becoming closer friends with his mentor.

He had so much respect for the older man and their growing friendship meant a lot to him.

He decided not to take notes that day – it would be rude – though he did hope he could remember it all later.

He did notice, however, before he left, that his notes seemed to be grouped into one of three categories: methodology, risk management, or psychology. And a failure in any one of these three areas would cause him to fail at trading.

Even if his trading method had a huge winning percent, if he didn't control his risk he would eventually lose the capital in his account either through one huge loss or too many losses in a row.

On the other hand, he could cut his losses like a professional every single time, but if he didn't have a method that was profitable historically or in the current market environment, he would not be successful in the long term.

If his system didn't have a strong winning edge over the market, his repetitive losses – combined with commission costs – would whittle down his account until it was ruined and too small to trade effectively.

He was also beginning to understand that even with a winning method and risk control he had to keep his head on straight.

After winning too many times in a row, his ego could get away from him, and he could easily trade too big a position size right when he was due for a loss and give back a large amount of profits in one trade, even while using his winning method and his risk control.

Another pitfall he knew to avoid was losing a few times in a row and then being too afraid to take a signal, ultimately missing out when the big winner finally arrived.

Or worse, he could experience several losses in a row which were simply due to occur on account of market changes, and this could cause him to lose faith in his method and system and abandon it altogether.

He had to make his trading plan with a clear mind and with clear thoughts before the trading day began; this trading plan had to give him an advantage over the market in long-term trading.

The probabilities of winning had to be on his side.

Trading was turning out to be harder than he expected. He realized there was much more to it than buying stocks which were going up. **Stock trading is not free money; profit must be earned through homework, discipline, courage, patience, and perseverance in the market.**

These were lessons he was learning loud and clear while dabbling in trading and reading stock-trader stories. He was also paper trading systems he was working on and studying charts.

He arrived at one of Rich Trader's favorite restaurants that evening. Rich Trader was seated at a large booth in the corner. He already had his first wine bottle on the table, along with some unfamiliar type of bread. Two small bowls of olive oil with herbs were set in the center of the table.

"Sit down and dig in. Order whatever you like; my treat."

New Trader thought this was very generous and looked over the menu carefully. He didn't want to be greedy with Rich Trader's money, but he really wanted a steak.

When the waiter arrived, New Trader was the first to order.

"I'd like the New York strip."

"And how would you like that cooked?"

Accustomed to fast food more than fancy restaurants, he had to think a moment.

"Well done," he finally responded.

"And I'd like the porterhouse – medium-rare," Rich Trader added.

As the waiter left, Rich Trader sensed New Trader's discomfort.

"You seem uncomfortable."

"Sorry, I can't help but think about how much this is going to cost."

"You're worried how much this is going to cost me? You have to stop thinking of money in those terms. You're probably calculating how many hours you would have to work to earn enough money to pay for this meal."

"Yes. I also hate to spend money. I'm always looking to save money, not spend it."

"While I agree that you should only spend money wisely, and frugality is a great way to get your first account for trading, I also believe it is important to enjoy the money you have earned and spend it on the things you find most important. While I couldn't care less about a new car or new computer, I like to spend my money on my home and dining with friends. When you spend money, you need to ask yourself if you are getting the value for the money that you are spending. If you are, then you should relax and enjoy it. If not, then don't spend your money that way again. But by all means, relax; these are trading profits well spent," said Rich Trader with a grin.

"In trading I really feel pain when I lose real money."

"Like we've talked about in the past, you have to understand – and then believe – that in your early trading your losses are your tuition to learning. It's no different than if you paid money to a college or to a technical school to get an education or training in your chosen career field. When you have advanced as a trader and have worked out your system, the losing trades are simply your cost of business; they will be paid for by your winning trades."

"When I lose, I feel like a failure – like I don't know what I'm doing."

"If you followed your trading plan 100% from start to finish, then it was a successful trade. If you made a mistake but learned a lesson from the trade, it was money well spent on tuition to improve your trading. Mistakes that lose real money tend to be remembered and corrected much more than money lost in paper trading or simulators."

"So what is the best way to deal with my stress when I'm losing money in a trade? I love winning but it still makes me sick to lose money."

"You have to look at dollars as points while you are trading. Professionals do not count their profits or losses while they are working. A doctor does not count how much he is making during surgery. 'Great, I made an incision, I just made $400; I'm removing the gall stone, that's another $800.' That is not how a professional operates in any field. They first focus on proper technique and the profits come later. Do not count your wins as they come because if you lose them it will hurt. Focus instead on following your system, taking your signals as you get them, and the profits will follow."

"How do I increase my chances for success in my system?"

"Let me think... I'll give you a top five list: How to improve the probabilities of your system becoming a winning system.

**1.**First, you want to trade with the market trend. You have much better odds if you are trading long in an uptrend and shorting in a down trend. The best way to determine this is to look at a chart of the S&P 500 or NASDAQ; if the 10-day moving average is above the 20-day moving average line, then you should be trading long in the uptrend. If the 10-day moving average is below the 20-day moving average, you are in a down trend. If the market is in an uptrend then you can follow a system where you go long based on your predetermined parameters. **But you have drastically lowered your probabilities of success trying to trade long as the market as a whole is going down. When a torpedo hits a ship, the whole ship sinks – not just part of it."**

"So I trade in sync with the overall market in whatever direction it is currently in?"

"That's step one...

**2.** You want to buy at the sweet spot on the chart for the stock or index. These are high consolidation areas where there is volume and a crossroad for decision. They include a breakout to a new all-time high where everyone has made money and have little interest in selling. A breakout could also be in a long-term resistance point like a 10-, 20-, or 50-day moving average which a price finally rises above. On the flip side, if you are shorting a stock when the price goes under the 20- or 50-day moving average, that is likely the place to go short since it indicates that it does not have buyers to support its price in the down trend. Sweet spots are also at a point of support on a chart in an uptrend; this could be the bottom of a Bollinger band which has held for a couple of months. The support could be at a specific moving average like the 10- or 20-day, or an actual price. It depends on the specific chart and your ability to see the repeating pattern to determine these areas. It is important to buy at that point after you have identified it through studying the chart. **Do not hesitate; buy it when your signal says to; do not wait and chase it after the fact.** If you wait and buy too late or too early, you lower the probability of your success."

"Yes. I need to take my signals, overcome fear, not be trigger-shy, and not be greedy and buy too soon. Got it," said New Trader, getting the feeling that Rich Trader repeated the same lessons over and over.

Rich Trader continued:

**3.** Do not trade based on your opinions or feelings. ONLY trade your system. Do not trade your system until you have both back tested it using software or eyeballing past charts and have a good idea of the win ratio and risk-versus-reward payout ratio. You will need at least 50 to 100 hypothetical trades for a reasonably accurate back test. You also need to test trade it on paper or a simulator to see how it performs in the current market and how you perform trading it. Then you are ready to trade. **In the stock market, opinions and feelings are wrong the majority of the time; however the current trend is right the majority of the time.** You have a very good chance of being right over the long term when you follow a proven system with discipline.

**4.** Becoming an expert in both specific stocks and in your chosen method puts you at an advantage. If you want to be a day trader you should understand how stocks trade during each hour increment of the day and know when the most volume is traded and when the market is most likely to trend. Your trading would be based on these observations. You might sit out the first hour because it was too choppy. Your system might simply be to buy breakouts after 2 p.m. on your watch list or buy off a bounce in support after 10:30

a.m. Your system might have you trade long while the major indexes are green, or short when they are red. Or your trade direction might be based on the weekly timeframe of whether they were above the 10-day moving average.

As an expert day trader, you would build a watch list of stocks which had price action that fit your trading system. If you were going to play day trends or breakouts, you would need volatile stocks with large daily average ranges. You would build watch lists of stocks based on these characteristics and become an expert on how they traded – their trends, average volume, the percent and dollar amounts they moved each day. You would know exactly when they had upcoming earnings announcements and everything that may affect their trading. You would change this list when you found better candidates than the ones you were trading. Someone who has studied something for hundreds if not thousands of hours will almost always beat someone with just a passing interest. There is a huge advantage to those who know what they are doing. **In the stock market, money flows from those who do not know how to trade to those who do.**

**5.** Follow the volume in your trading. The smart money knows where the action and profits are; find them. Monster stocks are not hidden under a rock; they are generally household names even before they go up an additional 200 to 500%. When a company has wild earnings expectations, traders and investors know about it. The price rises along with the volume. It is on the highest volume traded list on major web sites and in daily business newspapers. The funny thing is that in the past, many would-be traders looked for that hot penny stock or next obscure hot stock while drinking an energy drink produced by the next hot publicly traded company, or while listening to music on a new device called an iPod, made by the company whose stock became the biggest monster stock of that decade. Day traders increase the volumes of stocks which are perfect for day trading; option writers write options on equities which have movement that they can trade options on. Maximum volume flows into stocks and ETFs which have the greatest potential for successful trading. Trade these equities. Do not fall into the trap of hearing about some hot pick from a message board or a penny-stock-pumping newsletter. A lot of these sources are pumpers trying to get people to buy so they can sell what they already hold. Stay in the high traffic intersections where the volume is at. This will close the bid-and-ask spread so you do not lose money when you buy and sell, and you will always have a buyer ready to buy from you."

"So to summarize, to have a high probability of success in my trading I should:

1. Trade in the direction of the overall market trend only.
2. Let my system make all the trading decisions, not my opinions and feelings.
3. Buy only at the sweet spot on a chart.
4. Become an expert in the method I trade and on the stocks I trade on my watch list.
5. Trade where the volume is not in illiquid stocks or markets."

New Trader looked up at Rich Trader from where he was staring at his napkin. "Right?"

"That's how we win," responded Rich Trader as their food arrived.

"So this puts the odds on my side," New Trader mumbled. "Oh – could I have another napkin, please?"

"Of course," the waiter said pleasantly, leaving to retrieve it.

"These five dynamics working together are what can put

you in the 10% of traders who make money consistently and in the long term."

The waiter returned with a new napkin and New Trader stuffed his first one, packed with notes, into his pocket. He wished he'd brought that notebook now…

"Well, that's where I want to be, so that's just what I will have to do."

**"In the stock market and in Las Vegas, you make money on the difference between playing the true odds and the opponent's disregard of the odds." – Harvey Friedentag**

**Recommended reading for this chapter's lesson:**

High Probability Trading, by Marcel Link

## 14

### New Traders try to predict; Rich Traders follow what the market is telling them.

"So what do you think the market will do today?"

"I have no idea."

"Which stocks do you like?"

"The ones that go up."

"Are you long or short in the market?"

"My system has me long."

"Do you think this trend up will continue...?"

"I have no idea."

Rich Trader almost gritted his teeth.

"Do you think the job report coming out this morning will be good or bad?" New Trader asked, yet another attempt to get an opinion from his mentor.

"Not only do I not know but I also don't know if a good report will cause the uptrend to continue or if it will have traders selling the news. I do not predict, I do not have an opinion, and I really don't know. What I do know is that following trends makes me money, and my system captures the profits in trends and gets me out when it reverses."

"I'm still trying to wrap my brain around how a trader who does not predict prices makes money. Isn't predicting where prices are going the only way to make money?"

"First of all, that's impossible – the future hasn't happened yet, so how can it be predicted? Money is made by being right on the direction of your trade. The direction of the market or a stock generally stays in one overall trend with few changes the majority of the time. A stock, or the market, is usually in the process of making either a higher high price along with higher low prices over the short term, or lower high prices and lower low prices. This can usually be measured over any timeframe by checking the chart. This does not predict; it simply shows you the trend. You have better odds by simply going with the trend than trying to predict anything."

"So you read the market… you don't try to predict it?"

"Exactly – I read charts, I trade patterns, and I react to changes in trends. Most importantly, I follow the market. It tells me what to do. There is no way one person can predict what all market participants are going to do and figure that in with all the moving parts of the economy, world politics, and monetary policy. That's absurd. You throw in some random events and it's just luck if someone predicts correctly. The sad thing is that when someone calls some big event in advance, the majority of the time it was just a lucky call because someone was bound to be right with all the people making predictions. Of course, no one checks the records of how many times they were right in the past. They become a guru until their next few predictions don't come true and people move on to the next guru who is right on a big call."

"Okay, you don't believe in psychics in the stock market. I get it," said New Trader with a big smile.

"I do, however, know that traders can make money by following the market's direction. The whole point of creating your trading system is to develop signals which tell you when a trend begins and when it ends. The only signals you can use to determine a trend are price and volume. All other technical indicators are simply derivatives of these two. So you can make a system as complex as you want, but in my experience, I have seen people make millions and never even use the more complex technical indicators. Many of these new complex indicators were only invented in modern times with the help of computers. Few legendary traders of the last 100 years ever heard of these in their lifetime and they did fine. The tools I personally work with are price, volume, candlestick charts, and moving averages. That is just my personal choice; you should use any tool that helps you make money. Just limit your indicators to a manageable level so you don't confuse yourself. Three or four are usually plenty for anyone."

"So the purpose of the system I am building is to catch trends and to find common variables in the past that are identified at the beginning or end of a trend?"

"The price and volume of a stock reveal investor and trader behavior; human behavior never changes. It creates patterns you can observe. Greed and fear come into play in the markets and carry trends far beyond where rational fundamental valuations could ever take them. **The market is going to go where the votes carry it; your job is to vote with the majority.**"

**"The stock market is always right and always tells its own story best." – Benton Davis**

**Recommended reading for this chapter's lesson:**

You Can Still Make It in the Market, by Nicolas Darvas

## 15

## New Traders trade against the trend; Rich Traders follow the markets trend.

**"Trend":**

– Noun

1. The general course or prevailing tendency; drift: trends in the teaching of foreign languages; the trend of events.

2. Style; vogue: the new trend in women's apparel.

3. The general direction followed by a road, river, coastline, or the like.

– Verb (used without object)

4. To have a general tendency, as events, conditions, etc.

5. To tend to take a particular direction; extend in some direction indicated.

6. To veer or turn off in a specified direction, as a river, mountain range, etc.: The river trends toward the southeast.

– Related forms

coun•ter•trend, noun

sub•trend, noun

– Synonyms

1. See tendency, stretch, run, incline.


New Trader read through the definition of "trend" several times. He thought about what it really meant.

"The general course or prevailing tendency" really made sense to him – either the majority of investors were acquiring stock and holding for increasing profits or they were selling stocks because they were losing money and had fears of losing more.

Markets, stocks, and sectors all had general courses and a prevailing tendency in one direction or the other. In his study of charts, he actually saw more trends than range-bound charts.

It seemed like the majority of stock charts were making a run for a short-term high or low. Each stock was generally closer to the 52-week high or low, very rarely right in the middle.

He could usually identify up trends as stocks with a current price above a 10-day moving average and down trends in stocks because the current price was right at the 50-day moving average or under it.

It was also obvious to him that when the market as a whole was in an uptrend, most stocks were also in an uptrend.

He knew, of course, that there were stocks which were leaders and had the strongest up trends and other stocks which were laggards and in their own down trends, regardless of how strong the uptrend was in the general market.

What he was beginning to understand was that the leading stocks in the market had the best earnings expectations and the laggards had falling earnings because they were losing market share – or worse, they were losing money because their business model no longer worked. **Investment money flows where the earnings expectations grow.**

It was time for what was becoming his daily dose of Rich Trader. He wanted to hear Rich Trader's thoughts and experiences with the "trends" he continued to talk about.

New Trader and Rich Trader met at a lake almost exactly halfway between their houses.

New Trader showed up just as the sun peaked out. He felt the warmth seeping into his skin as he waited comfortably on a bench, a few small children skipping rocks nearby.

Rich Trader approached moments later, and they smiled at each other – it seemed they both had the same idea, bringing a loaf of bread with them.

But then again, it was more of a defensive measure, as these ducks were aggressive. The ducks and geese weren't at all shy, pecking and quacking at their visitors for bread. They were spoiled things, really.

"What are the best ways to identify and trade trends?" New Trader began, after a few minutes of throwing bits of bread towards the approaching ducks.

"You search for increasing volume; you look for the highest volume stocks and ETFs and look for new recent high and new low prices. Ideally, you would like to see an equity you're interested in trading which has been in a tight price range for a few months; like, say a low of $95 and a high of $100 suddenly break to a new all-time high of $101 on twice the average daily volume. That is a trend right from birth. Sellers are no longer willing to give up their stock at $100, and buyers are willing to pay $101 because they believe it will go up for whatever reason and they will make money. Trend traders do not care why it is going up; trend traders only care that it is. As a matter of fact, trend traders are not bullish or bearish; they do not care which direction the market is moving, only that it is moving. The trend trader's system would have been just as likely to sell the same stock short at $94 as he would have been to go long at $101. Many trend traders became millionaires following simple systems that used price alone as the trigger to buy and sell. They traded both stocks and commodities that were trending in nature and capitalized on this."

Rich Trader had been tossing bread throughout his speech – the ducks seemed hungrier than usual, and that was saying something.

"And what causes trends?"

"For one, supply and demand –for the stock, with increasing buyers driving up the price, or for the company's product, which drives up earnings and brings in more buyers hoping to profit from the fundamentals.

"The human emotions of greed and fear can also drive equities to overshoot fundamental valuations by absurd amounts. In a down trend, fear increases with each tick downward in price. Investors lose money and throw in the towel when they lost large amounts of money in their accounts. At the same time other traders short the stock after seeing the price fall, in anticipation of making money on the fall. Down trends feed on losses as buyers have a hard time buying when all they see is that others are losing money."

Rich Trader took a breath and gave another piece of bread to a duck that seemed to be almost territorial.

"Up trends also turn into growing fires, and the gasoline of greed sparks more buyers to jump on board as a stock rockets upward. Fearful of losing out on a big run up, traders wait for a pullback give up and buy. Others who sold the stock short have to cover by buying it back, adding even more buying pressure to the uptrend."

These ducks are not normal, New Trader couldn't help but think as he listened to Rich Trader. They seemed so much more docile in his youth…

**"A trend trader only has to catch the meat of a trend to make money and be right; a counter trend trader has the odds stacked against him because he has to pick a big reversal on the top or bottom to be right."**

"Do I have to buy new highs as a trend trader?"

"No, not at all, as long as you can establish that the equities on your watch list are in an uptrend, you could also buy on pullbacks. You can measure pullbacks by looking at charts for support. Your stock may have support at the 10-day moving average or 20-day moving average over the past two months. If you can verify that in the past the price finds support at the 20-day moving average and then goes back up, your system could consist of buying at the 20-day moving average. You then have to decide when you want to sell. Depending on the strength of the trend, you can let it ride as long as it does not lose the 20-day again, or you may sell when it reaches the top of a Bollinger Band. It depends on that particular stock's chart. In a strong up trend sometimes the 10- and 20-day moving averages are not touched by the price for weeks. The moving average grows bigger so when your stop is triggered you have a profit because the moving average price you sell at is much larger than when you bought it. You may also have a stock, as we discussed earlier, bouncing around in a slow up trend with a low of $95 and a high of $100 for weeks on end. Your system could be to buy at the support around $95 and sell at resistance of $100. You can use price as well as moving averages for support and resistance. You just want to be sure to buy as the stock bounces up off resistance rather than falls through it. The perfect buy off a bounce-off support in an uptrend would be for it to hit $95.05, and then go up to $95.50; that would be a buy off support. If it hit $94.75, then fell to $94.25, you do not want any part of it; that is a fall through support."

"So a system can buy off different signals in an uptrend, not only a new high. But I suppose I want to take signals that make me long in a bull market and short in a bear market."

"Exactly – a good way to lose money is to go short in a bull market or long in a bear market; the probabilities are stacked against you. It is very arrogant to think you can call tops, bottoms, and market reversals. The only thing traders should be trying to do is call the market direction and decide where to stop their losses when it reverses."

"What percentage of the time do trend traders win?" asked New Trader, expecting an impossibly high 90%.

"The best trend traders' wins are between 40 to 50 percent. What makes them successful is that when they win they win big and when they lose they lose small. The drawback is that they have losing periods during choppy markets where they lose many times in a row. However over the long term their wins compound and their equity grows to amazing amounts."

"Sounds like you speak from personal experience," said New Trader, smiling as he flung bread to one of the ducks that seemed to never be satisfied – although that was pretty much all of them.

"Yes, I have benefited like many others from trend trading over a long period of time. The hardest part may be to keep faith in your system when it suffers several losses in a row. It also gets more difficult as your capital grows larger and larger. A $100,000 trade feels different than a $10,000 trade."

"I wish I had that problem," New Trader said with a laugh.

"I trade a system that is purely technical; it was created based on past performance. My system only depends on the actual trend, not my opinions or news stories. I do not trade off fundamental values; I trade off other traders' and investors' reactions in buying and selling. I do not predict the trend, I follow the trend. I measure the trend through volume, price, and moving averages."

"Trading is rocket science – you find a rocket and ride it."

**"There is only one side to the stock market, not the bull side or the bear side, but the right side. It took me longer to get that general principle fixed firmly in my mind than it did most of the more technical phases of the game of stock market speculation." – Jesse Livermore**

**Recommended reading for this chapter's lesson:**

Trend Following, by Michael Covel

## 16

## New Traders follow their emotions, which put them at a disadvantage; Rich Traders follow systems that give them an advantage.

Over the next month New Trader studied charts. He studied stocks and their behavior. He had a watch list of five stocks that he believed were the hottest in the market at the time.

They all had five characteristics:

1. They were within 5% of all-time highs in price.
2. They each traded over five million shares a day, some much more.
3. They all had new types of products or business models that were successful.
4. Each of them had earnings increases of over 20% year over year for the same quarter – some much more.
5. All the companies were expected to continue to grow in sales and profits and take over or change the market place.

This was the fundamental part of his trading plan that would determine his watch list and what he would trade.


All of New Trader's stocks were in established up trends, with each month in the past six months having higher prices than the previous month's high prices.

None of the stocks on his watch list had lost their 50-day moving averages in the past six months. They generally stayed above the 20-day moving average, touching it only in market retracements. These stocks spent over 80% of their time above the 10-day moving average, going to new high prices around each of the last two earnings announcements.

He also set up Bollinger Bands on his charts with the setting of a 20-day moving average and two standard deviations. These stocks also spent much of their time scraping their price along the top of their Bollinger Bands. He noticed that many of the stocks in down trends scraped across the bottom of Bollinger Bands, and these down trending stocks were almost the reverse of his watch list; on their charts the 10-day moving average was below the 20-day moving average, which was also below the 50-day moving average.

He wanted his system to capture the up trends in the strongest stocks. It looked to him like the 10-day moving average was a great support in up trends and resistance in down trends.

His study also led him to believe that the top Bollinger Band was resistance in up trends and the bottom band was support in down trends. Not always, of course, but most of the time.

He looked at charts with up trends:

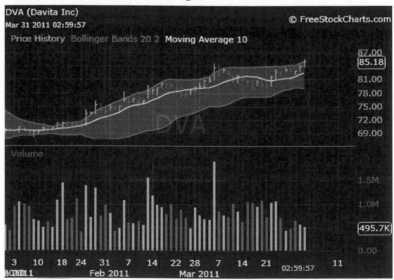

He looked at up trends that turned into down trends:

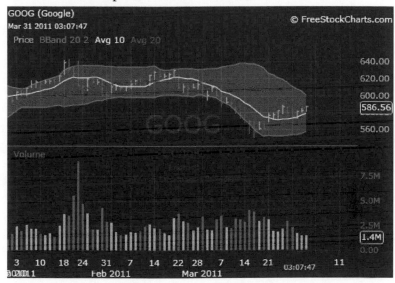

Volatile stocks:

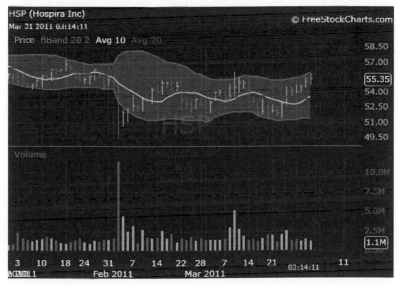

Nice up trends:

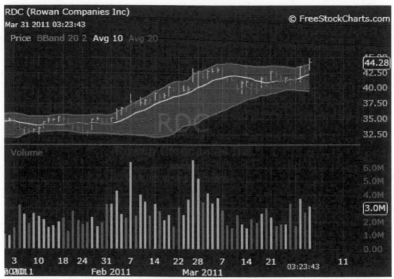

Strong up trends:

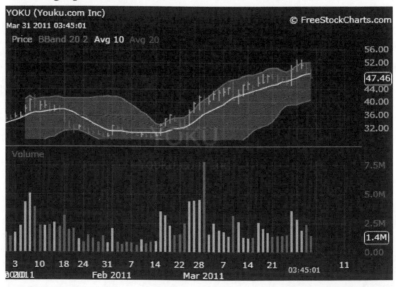

New Trader only wanted to trade stocks that had charts with solid stable up trends in price. He decided it would be to nerve racking for him to trade stocks that had prices with large daily price swings.

Volatility was not going to be his friend in trend trading systems; it would cause false stop losses to be triggered when the stock broke below support for a moment and also early profit taking when the price reversed momentarily below the trailing stop likely to only retrace back up to where it was before the momentary retracement. A volatile stock could lose its 10-day moving average one day and the next day be back up above it again.

New Trader wanted stocks where 10-day moving averages held up for at least 20 trading days. He saw a lot of opportunity in buying stocks on his watch list at the 10-day moving average and selling when the 10-day moving average was breached and not recovered before the close.

In up trending stocks, by the time the 10-day was breached it could have run up 20% in price or more.

While the top Bollinger Bands were resistance, it would not be wise to sell as they penetrated the top band since the stocks on his watch list tended to stay at the top band and keep going up.

He could really let profits run with a 10-day moving average so rarely breached on the stocks on his watch list.

He felt confident that he was on the right path in effective system building. His technical rules would be:

1. New trader would buy stocks on his watch list as they trended up through the 10-day moving average or bounced off it as support.

2. After he made the buy he would set a stop loss 2% below his purchase price. This would put only 2% of his capital at risk at any time during his trade.

3. Once his buy was correct and his stock started trending upwards and reached 2% above the 10-day moving aver-

age he would then set the stop at the current 10-day moving average, moving it up or down based on the newly figured 10 moving average each day. The popular moving average would be his trailing stop loss to lock in profits and be his signal to sell because the trend had reversed.

4. This system went for the home runs, not taking profits until the uptrend ended. This system also seemed to play it safe, getting out before any large losses could ensue after the loss of support.

5. Of his $10,000 account he would trade $2,500 per trade. He knew this would take a lot of the emotions out of his trades and let him focus on the system, not the profits. He would move up in size as his equity grew. This would also help with risk; these stocks could experience the 'torpedo' effect and fall quickly if they missed earnings or lowered guidance. It took a large supply of helium to keep these balloons floating so high in the air. While they could go up they could also pop and come down. It would be very important to control position size and stop losses at the 10-day moving average.

New Trader believed this was a sound system, and his buy point would be important; he didn't want to be whip-sawed if it fell 2% right when he bought it.

He believed this system would perform very well in real trading as long as the market as a whole stayed in an uptrend. He had also come to know the reality of trading and how different it was when real money was on the line and a stock did not move upwards in price like he believed it would.

These thoughts caused him to go back and add one more rule:

6. He would only trade this system when the S&P 500 chart had the 10-day moving average above the 20-day moving average and the price of the S&P 500 was above the 20-day moving average.

The market needed to be in an overall up trend and bullish for his system to be consistently profitable. He believed this rule would help his odds substantially.

Now he felt as if he had built a system that would work and enable him to trade with control over his emotions and limited risk.

He believed he had an advantage now. He thought all the books he had read and all the talks with Rich Trader were beginning to come together for him.

Oddly enough, he got the most value from looking at charts for hours on end. That was reality; no opinions; only stock price and trading volume action.

He now knew there was a flow and ebb – almost a rhythm – to the stock market.

He could almost visualize traders making decisions inside the charts he looked at. He could imagine them letting their profits run as stocks shot upwards in price, going higher and higher with little selling pressure.

He noticed fear in some charts as the uptrend was broken and a stock quickly fill to its 20-day moving average and after a last gasp tumbled down to the bottom Bollinger Band, where other traders were waiting patiently to grab the bargain they sought.

He now believed that moving averages and Bollinger Bands were sometimes self-fulfilling prophecies.

He did not believe that the indicators, in themselves, had any real power, but the traders' belief in them led to the buy and sell decisions that he watched play out in the charts.

It looked like traders loved to add to positions at the 10-day moving average over and over again. Also the 20-day, 50-day, and even 100-day moving averages seemed to be places on charts where traders made the decision to buy to support prices or sell when these supports were broken.

He wondered if mutual fund managers have huge piles of cash sitting on the sideline just waiting to enter these stocks on pullbacks.

New Trader was beginning to feel like he was not trading stocks but trading on others' opinions of a stock's price and movement, and he realized the worst mistake he could make was trying to trade against the majority's opinion.

New Trader believed his new system would capture up trends in the hottest stocks in the market, and his watch list would be based on stocks of great growing companies – not his opinions, but businesses which already excelled in earnings increases and future expectations of more of the same.

He would trade only if the stocks still had great price charts and investor interest. The most important thing was that he would time his buys at high probability points which from a historical perspective seemed profitable.

He believed he had built a solid plan and system for up trends. But the big question was: Would Rich Trader approve?

**"The sooner you realize you are trading against other traders and not just the stocks or the market, the better off you will be." – Quint Tatro**

**Recommended reading for this chapter's lesson:**
The Complete Turtle Trader, by Michael Covel

## 17

### New Traders do not know when to cut losses or lock in gains; Rich Traders have an exit plan.

New Trader had given Rich Trader a couple of weeks off from mentoring; he was trying not to become an annoyance.

One of the greatest things about talking to Rich Trader was that he was given tools he could use to develop himself as a trader.

Rich Trader was not going to tell him what to do; he was going to show him how to do it.

Trading style and trading system are very personal choices which have to fit a trader's tolerance of risk and pain.

Just because a system worked well for Rich Trader did not mean New Trader could just use and succeed at it too. Just like jobs must be a good fit in order for a worker to succeed, trading has to fit the trader.

While styles of trading could differ and systems could have different buy and sell signals, it was the principles of trading which New Trader was learning that had to be the same. Many of these were principles not just for trading but for business and success in life as well.

As New Trader approached Rich Trader's house he felt different. He couldn't put his finger on exactly what was different. Was he just in a good mood?

He felt he had much more control over his trading. He did not feel obsessed with having to trade. His only goal was to make money, not prove anything.

If he was going to have to cut a loss it was simply because the market was not currently conducive to his system of profit making. He was not wrong; he just had to take a loss.

After so many hours of pouring over charts he was confident that over the long term he would make money with his system.

He also knew that his losses would probably come from being stopped out 50% of the time, but his wins would come from huge moves in a stock he would not be able to predict. He could only follow the action.

He felt confident, he felt calm, and he felt like he was becoming a real trader rather than just talking to one – he was a peer.

He believed he was ready to start his career in the markets in a disciplined and focused manner.

"Long time no see," Rich Trader said as he answered the door. "I was starting to think you gave up."

"Give up?" New Trader grinned. "I was just giving you a vacation!"

"I have been asked to mentor many others over the years and nine out of ten give up very quickly. Most don't even meet for a second time. Their heads spin from all the information. All they really want is easy money. **The one thing I have learned in my decades in the market is that there is no easy money laying around for traders on Wall Street.** Believe me, I've searched everywhere. There may not be any easy money on this earth. Unless you work for the government," added Rich Trader very seriously before laughing.

"Business is business, whether I'm trading stocks or delivering pizza. I believe that now. Success at anything in life requires controlling risk, the right mindset, a successful method, supply and demand, discipline, courage, stopping losses, and letting winners run."

"The funny thing is that the principles you have been teaching me for trading success have also been helping me in other areas of my life. I think much more clearly about many parts of my life now. My journal has expanded into a self-help journal as well as a trading journal. I did not even think about many of these things until after I learned many of the principles we've been discussing. I would like to read you some thoughts from my journal and see what you think."

New Trader believed that his self-improvement would help with his trading and that he had really ingested the principles Rich Trader was trying to instill in him because not only did he understand their application for trading, but he applied them to other areas of his life.

New Trader began reading, excited to finally share these observations with his mentor.

- In life, as in trading, the right mindset is crucial for success. You must be confident in your decisions because they are based on cause and effect, not on emotions or opinion. Negative people who are unsure of themselves are not successful in any field. You need faith in yourself and your methods to be able to persevere and not give up before reaching success.

- You can risk too much and lose it all in your business, life, marriage, friendships or family. You have to measure the potential cost of every action. One affair can cost you your marriage, just like one big trade with too much risk can cost you all your capital.

- In business there are certain methods which bring in customers and turn a profit, and others which cause a business to turn away customers and lose money. Trading is similar: methods which turn a consistent and long-term profit are essential for success.

- Having unrealistic expectations in a marriage, job, or business will lead to unhappiness and failure just like it will in trading. You have to set realistic expectations so you do not get discouraged easily and quit in any of these areas. You have to be satisfied that the results are worth your effort over the long term. You need to understand what to expect before you begin a marriage, a job, a business, or trading.

- Those who succeed in all areas of life are the ones who can manage stress the best. The best way to manage stress is to increase what you can handle step by step so that you grow into new circumstances. Another way to manage stress is to avoid actions which get you into situations you are uncomfortable with.

- Patience can pay big dividends in life. Patience is not inaction; it is simply knowing what you are looking for and taking action at the right time. Whether you are waiting for the right trade setup or the right person to marry, **patience can protect you from irrational emotions and feelings.** Wait for what you want, and when it is there go get it.

- In life, as in trading, people with written plans accomplish much more than people with no plans. Sit down when you are calm and rational and jot down goals to pursue. This will provide you with a map when life circumstances bring out your fears, greed, and other destructive emotions.

- Education does not end in school. To be successful in life or trading we must never stop learning. The market and the world are constantly advancing and changing and the only way to keep up is to keep learning.

- In life, the majority of gamblers are broke and the majority of good business owners become rich. The same principle is true in trading.

- In life, if you risk everything enough times you will eventually lose everything. Instead, just **move in the direc-**

**tion of your goals every day, so even with setbacks, in the long run you will get to where you are going.**

- Before making any decision in life, the question: "What do I have to lose?" is a serious question. This should precede, "What do I have to gain?" If the answer is: I could lose $100, but if I am right I could gain $500 and my odds of being right are 50% – then you have a good risk reward profile. If it is reversed, then you have a bad risk reward scenario and should pass. These are also questions you must ask in your marriage, job, business, or friendships before making decisions you regret.

- Failure to admit when you are wrong can be disastrous. When you are going down the wrong road it is better to turn back sooner rather than later. Never fight a war for a hill of bones, because even if you win, all you have is a hill of bones and regret over what it cost you.

- When you have won big prepare to take profits. Have an exit plan in place. If your house goes from $100,000 to $300,000, have a plan to sell and move. Do not just sit there and let it drop back down to $100,000. It is surprising how many people are in the right place at the right time and win what is equivalent to the lottery in stocks, a house, or a business but have no exit plan, so they ride it all the way up then all the way down again with almost nothing to show for it. Tragic.

- What most separates successful people from unsuccessful people in all areas of life is that they persevere until they are successful. Everyone has to overcome failures, but those who keep going are the ones with successful marriages, businesses, careers, and trading systems.

- People who are successful become experts in one area. They put in 10 years of learning and mastering one business, one career, one marriage, or one trading style. They do not jump around and become a jack-of-all-trades and master of none.

- Successful people do what really leads to success, not what they believe will make them successful. They read books, study patterns, have mentors, and learn cause and effect.

- Winners base their actions on proven results, not on their own opinions or predictions. Feedback is crucial to them; people with strong opinions who believe they can predict what will happen reject feedback. Winners go with the flow of the trend causing their success.

- In life, those who are driven by their vision, passion, and plan usually end up where they want to be or close to it. Those who let their emotions and feelings take over and drive their decision-making usually end up where they do not want to be in life.

- I believe that people who realize they have made a mistake in a given situation and who cut those losses and try again will be much more successful than people who waste years on a marriage, business, or career that continuously gets worse. It is important to continue in a business or career that is successful until that trend changes.

"I see you've been listening. I think you may be starting to teach me a few things. I'm very impressed."

"Thanks. It's all starting to come together for me. You've really made me think about the importance of the trader in any trading system and aware of many principles of success that I really never even thought about before. What's been the most difficult thing for you as a trader?"

"I have always hated losing money. I hate taking a loss. It used to make me feel bad. Now I realize it is the cost of doing business, but I don't like it. But what really hurt back when I was a young trader was not taking that first stop loss and allowing a small loss to turn into a large one. That really made me sick. My first year of trading, I planned to get out with a $100 loss. I thought I was lucky because twice I did not take a loss. I watched a $115 loss go back to even and then a $150 loss turn into a $100 profit, so this emboldened me. It actually turned out that I was not lucky; I was unlucky because it took me longer to discipline myself to take the first loss. I had a hard time not thinking that I would get lucky again, so let it ride, it would come back. The next time I was down $100 I abandoned my plan and thought I was smart enough to read the price and volume action and make a decision. The problem was that a young trader in this situation is only going to see what he wants to see. I didn't want to take the loss at first; then I didn't want to be wrong about not taking it.

Then I committed the final deadly sin of a trader: I really hoped it would get back to even. This was the worst trade I ever made. I turned what should have been a trade of a few days for a $300 profit into a weeklong ordeal that turned a $100 loss into a $500 loss. Not to mention the ridiculous time I wasted glued to its every tick. I rode an emotional roller coaster of hope as it rebounded 50 cents, then a wave of despair as it fell back and made a lower low. I did not know there were rumors in the company about a product that was going to have to be recalled. But I didn't need to know; I just needed to follow my rules and get out. That was a good lesson which taught me from then on to honor my stops when they were hit the first time. **The first planned stop loss is the best one to follow.** I promised I would never do that to myself again.

I believe this is good practice in life as well as trading. It saves your most precious resource – time. It also avoids emotional wear and tear on your psyche and stomach lining. These are important resources you will need for a long trading career..."

"A loss never bothers me after I take it. I forget it overnight. But being wrong – not taking the loss – that is what does damage to the pocketbook and to the soul." – Jesse Livermore

**Recommended reading for this chapter's lesson:**

Wall Street: the Other Las Vegas, by Nicolas Darvas

## 18

### New Traders cut profits short and let losses run; Rich Traders let profits run and cut losses short.

Rich Trader was looking over New Trader's system.

New Trader's visits were now occurring only every other week instead of several times a week. Months had passed since New Trader had reached out for guidance from Rich Trader.

Though regular visits were getting fewer and fewer, this was not a sign of a lack of drive. New Trader spent about two hours a day, every day, looking at charts, studying his watch list, and reading the best trading books he could find.

He felt Rich Trader had given him the basic tools and he was now building his trading skills.

At first he was like many traders – very disappointed that Rich Trader did not show him the holy grail of trading which guaranteed profits.

He also expected a multi-screen set up with CNBC in the background and Rich Trader frantically trading on every piece of news.

This was not how he traded, nor was it how the legends he researched traded. While Rich Trader never said it was wrong, New Trader started to believe that the only way to go was trend following.

This was his style of choice. This is where he saw the money and the potential.

New Trader waited patiently as Rich Trader continued to look over his trading plan and system along with the records of his paper trades he had brought.

"Your winning ratio looks very good – 60%. That's excellent. However, your system was benefiting from the recent up trend in the market. Your losses were small due to your tight stops, but that may be too tight; you could experiment with 3% under the 10-day moving average as your stop or even use a 12- or 14-day moving average as a better indicator. When the market turns choppy or at the beginning of a down trend it will affect your winning ratio a great deal. But it will also give you fewer trades, as the 10-day moving average will likely become resistance and give very few buy signals. I also believe your system will take you safely to cash in a major market retracement. This is a very good plan."

New Trader was so set on the 10-day and 20-day moving averages that he had never even considered any others.

What a simple suggestion; how had he not thought of that? It would become a whole different chart if he changed the moving averages. What if another moving average showed more reaction than the 10 or 20 day? This was a very interesting idea to look into.

"Your payoff ratio was a little over 2:1. You made about $200 in profits for every $100 in losses. This is excellent; it will be less when you really begin to trade and have to figure in the difference of the bid/ask spread when entering and exiting trades along with commissions and slippage, where you do not get the price you want as easily as you do in paper trading, especially with market orders on stocks with lower volume at different parts of the trading day. But a payoff ratio of 1.5:1 is still a very robust and profitable system in which you should do well in the long term, especially during bull markets."

"Yes, paper trading is like shooting a fish in a barrel. I'm ready to start building a real trading record. I think it's ready to go live."

"Your largest winning trade was $500 and your largest losing trade was $125. That looks very good. This is an amazing return for a $2,500 trade. You had a $25 stock move up to $30 without touching the 10-day moving average? You are definitely trading stocks with good momentum and investor interest."

"I sold the big winner at $30 when it pulled back to the 10-day moving average on the chart; it pulled back to $30 after a runaway trend. It ran up before the company's earnings announcement to as high as $33.50. My system actually had me sell this stock and take profits before the announcement; it crashed back to $25 after the earnings were announced. This makes me want to add a rule that I do not hold through earnings. The trend can go either way dramatically after these high fliers announce their earnings for the quarter. The stocks that I trade can even crash in price after their company's report blows out earnings above expectations; it is just a matter of when the stock runs out of new buyers, and if the great earnings are all ready baked into the stock's price."

"That would be a great rule to better manage risk and volatility. While you will give up some huge profits, sometimes you will also avoid the extreme risk and equity draw downs by holding through an event with an unknown outcome. **I always put capital preservation before capital appreciation.** When I traded individual stocks I only held through earnings once and that was a disaster. In my personal trading, I had much better risk adjusted returns playing the expectation of earnings leading up to the announcement than holding through earnings. It was like the Wild West in the market after an earnings announcement. It was very unpredictable."

"Your average winning trade was $212," Rich Trader continued, "and your average losing trade was $105. These are very good numbers. So you returned 42.6% on your $10,000 in capital in 50 trades? That's astounding; unfortunately real trading will shave that down dramatically. When you go to really trade the market may enter a bear market at the very moment you start trading this system, causing many stops to be hit in a row and several losses. Then commissions will take a bite out of every trade, especially with your trading size. Twenty dollars in commission on a $2,500 trade is 0.8% on that capital before you even know if you win or lose. You need to trade with a per share broker who charges $1 per 100 shares, not one who charges $10 per trade or your account will be eaten up with commissions. You will also experience technical problems at the worst possible times with your computer, the Internet, power supply, or your broker's web site or trading platform. Rest assured that when this happens you may miss a great trade which would have made you a lot of money. You will also place market orders that are filled at worse prices than you expected; it will be unexpected, hurt your returns, and make you angry."

"So a 42.6% return in 50 trades may be a little too good to be true. If you get a bigger account size or a cheaper broker I believe your system is an excellent starting point. I would expect a return of about 19% during up trending bull markets after considering all these other factors. Your system will likely lose at the beginning of a bear market until it no longer has buy signals and until the next up trend begins."

New Trader had a lot to think about. He knew what Rich Trader said was true. It was disheartening, but it was reality.

"Would you suggest I develop a second system to trade in a bear market?"

"If you like; some traders do not like shorting, ever. They simply play whatever is going up. Some would rather buy only stocks in up trends in bear markets like gold miners, oil stocks, consumer staples, energy stocks, dollar stores, discount stores, or just stay in cash and wait. That is a personal choice. I go short when I get my signals to short."

"That would double my chances to make money…"

"It also doubles your chances to lose money," Rich Trader replied with a half smile.

"So I am at my starting point? I am ready to begin real trading?"

"You're more than ready. What's left is to let the markets teach you; they give great instant feedback and are never wrong. Prices are always what they should be at any given moment. Prices are the composite of what every buyer and seller agrees to pay at that moment."

"I don't know if I'm graduating from stock trading college or stock trading boot camp."

"Well, one thing is for sure. You are going to battle others for profits. If you do all the things you have learned, you will profit from others' mistakes."

New Trader made a decision that day. He would keep trading until he was successful.

He was no longer a new trader; he was a trend trader.

**"It's not whether you're right or wrong that's important, but how much money you make when you're right and how much you lose when you're wrong." – George Soros**

**Recommended reading for this chapter's lesson:**

How I made $2,000,000 in the Stock Market, by Nicolas Darvas

## Appendix A

## Recommended Resources for Traders

Newspaper

Investor's Business Daily

Web Sites:

www.DarvasTrader.com (subscribe to the newsletter)

www.chartpattern.com

www.investors.com

www.Investimonials.com (Reviews of all things financial)

www.Amazon.com (Trading Book reviews)

www.freestockcharts.com

Suggested Follows on Twitter:

@DanZanger

@DarvasTrader

@IBDInvestors

## Appendix B

## Author's Trading Results 2003-2010

Steve Burns has not had a losing year actively trading in his two main accounts since 2002. From 2003-2007 he returned an average annual gain of 22.95% and went to a cash position on January 4th, 2008, keeping all of his stock market profits through the Great Panic. His trading beat the S&P 500 for six straight years and had a cumulative 209.5% return over an eight-year period. His returns averaged 15.7% versus the S&P, returning 7.8% from 2003-2010.

The author trades accounts worth over a quarter of a million dollars. These accounts were built using the principles contained in this book.

## Appendix C

## My Top Ten Trading Book Recommendations for New Traders

#1 Trading for a Living by Alexander Elder

#2 The Universal Principles of Successful Trading by Brent Penfold

#3 Super Trader by Van K. Tharp

#4 A Trader's Money Management System by Bennett A. McDowell

#5 Trading without Gambling by Marcel Link

#6 Wall Street: The Other Las Vegas by Nicolas Darvas

#7 You Can Still make It in The Market by Nicolas Darvas

#8 How I Made Money using the Nicolas Darvas System by Steve Burns

#9 Overcoming 7 Deadly Sins of Trading by Ruth Barrons Roosevelt

#10 Twelve Habitudes of Highly Successful Traders by Ruth Barrons Roosevelt

**Appendix D**

## My Top Ten Trading Book Recommendations to Make You a Rich Trader

#1 Trend Following by Michael Covel

#2 How to Make Money in Stocks by William O'Neil

#3 Come into my Trading Room by Alexander Elder

#4 How I Made $2,000,000 in the Stock Market by Nicolas Darvas

#5 Market Wizards by Jack Schwager

#6 Reminiscences of a Stock Operator by Edwin Lefevre

#7 Lessons from the Greatest Stock Traders of All Time by John Boik

#8 How to Trade in Stocks by Jesse Livermore

#9 The Complete Turtle Trader by Michael Covel

#10 Monster Stocks by John Boik

## Appendix E

## My Top Ten Book Recommendations for Success in Life and Trading

#1 The Top Ten Distinctions between Winners and Whiners by Keith Cameron Smith

#2 The Total Money Makeover by Dave Ramsey

#3 Financial Peace by Dave Ramsey

#4 Rich Dad, Poor Dad by Robert Kiyosaki

#5 The Power of Now by Eckhart Tolle

#6 Unlimited Power by Tony Robbins

#7 The Top Ten Distinctions between Millionaires and the Middle Class by Keith Cameron Smith

#8 Harmonic Wealth by James Arthur Ray

#9 The Anatomy of Success by Nicolas Darvas

#10 Creating your Best Life by Caroline Adams & Dr. Michael Frisch

## About the Author

*Steve Burns* has been an active and successful trader for over 12 years. He is the author of "How I Made Money Using the Nicolas Darvas System" published by BN Publishing (available at all major Internet retailers). Mr. Burns ranks in the top 300 of all reviewers on Amazon.com; he is also one of the site's top reviewers for books on trading. He has been featured as a top Darvas System trader on DarvasTrader.com. He is also a contributor to ZenTrader.ca. His trading book reviews have been featured on BusinessInsider.com. His account outperformed the S&P 500 for six straight years during 2003-2008 with over a 20% return each of those years and has not had a losing year since 2002. He lives in Nashville, TN with his wife, Marianne, and they have five children: Nicole, Michael, Janna, Kelli, and Joseph, and one granddaughter, Alyssa.

*Contact Steve:*
E-Mail: stephenburns@bellsouth.net
Facebook: Steve Burns Nashville, TN
Twitter: @SJosephBurns
Contributor to: ZenTrader.ca
Contributor to: BusinessInsider.com
Contributor to: Oxstones Investment Club
Top Reviewer: Amazon.com
Member of Amazon.com/Vine Program

## Acknowledgements

I would like to thank Uri at BN Publishing for giving me the opportunity to write two books. This was a goal that I did not think I would accomplish until after I retired. The first book was an opportunity to show that the Darvas System does work. This book is an opportunity to give new traders a head start in a simple and easy-to-understand format without bogging them down with 300 pages of filler words. I hope traders find it useful and use the book as a starting point in their trading careers.

I also want to thank my wife Marianne for always believing in my trading even though she only wanted to hear about the bottom-line profits, not the amounts of money I traded. She has given me the freedom to create an up trend in our capital over the past seven years and did not worry about the brief draw downs.

I could not have written this book with out my co-author and daughter Janna. She loves writing like I love trading. She turned my concrete blocks of text into a story. She can also talk trading with the best of them.

## References

The North American Securities Administrators Association did a study and found that 11.5% of traders were profitable, 18.5% were breaking even, and 70% lost money

**Web Sites:**

www.contrarianvalueinvesting.com

www.brainyquote.com

http://stock-market.superiorinvestor.net

www.traders-talk.com

http://trenders.blogspot.com

http://2.bp.blogspot.com/_C0Jf4qaV4-8/S2JwqY-OQIJI/AAAAAAAAAKk/kTXcIwIL0Bg/s1600-h/S%26P+500+1989-2009.JPG (S&P 500 annual returns)

http://en.wikipedia.org/wiki/Cuban_Revolution

http://www.investopedia.com/terms

www.Chartpatterns.com

http://dictionary.reference.com/browse/trend_

http://www.seertrading.com

FreeStockCharts.com

**Books:**

"Trade the Trader" – Quint Tatro

# Recommended Reading

How I made $2,000,000 in the Stock Market
*By: Nicolas Darvas*

Wall Street: The Other Las Vegas
*By: Nicolas Darvas*

You Can Still Make it in the Market
*By: Nicolas Darvas*

How I Made Money Using the Nicolas Darvas System,
Which Made Him $2,000,000 in the Stock Market
*By Steve Burns*

The Battle for Investment Survival
*by Gerald M. Loeb*

The Psychology Of The Stock Market
*by G. C. Selden*

The Science of Getting Rich
*by Wallace D. Wattles*

Think and Grow Rich
*by Napoleon Hill*

TRADING SMART: 92 Tools, Methods, Helpful Hints and
High Probability Trading Strategies to Help You Succeed at
Forex, Futures, Commodities and Stock Market Trading
*By Jim Wyckoff*

Rules Used by Profitable Traders for Investing in Gold and Silver
*By Arik Zahb*

## *Available at www.bnpublishing.net*

Printed in Great Britain
by Amazon.co.uk, Ltd.,
Marston Gate.